THE BLACK PANTHER

Donald Neilson. (Hawkes, *The Capture of the Black Panther*)

THE BLACK PANTHER

THE TRIALS AND ABDUCTIONS OF DONALD NEILSON

GORDON LOWE

The
History
Press

In memory of Lesley Whittle

~&

First published 2016

The History Press
The Mill, Brimscombe Port
Stroud, Gloucestershire, GL5 2QG
www.thehistorypress.co.uk

British Library Cataloguing in Publication Data.
A catalogue record for this book is available from the British Library.

ISBN 978 0 7509 6738 9

Typesetting and origination by The History Press
Printed and bound in Great Britain by TJ International Ltd

1

Mrs Dorothy Whittle arrived back home just before one o'clock on the morning of Tuesday, 14 January 1975 after a pleasant evening with her friends. Widowed now for nearly five years, she made sure there was something to occupy her on most evenings – her friends at the club to start the week, at home with her 17-year-old daughter Lesley on Tuesday evenings, bingo on Wednesdays, and so on. Life had always been busy for her. First as George Whittle's secretary, then his common-law wife when he split up with his wife, and years helping him run the family coach business he'd successfully built up into the fourth largest in the country. Not forgetting her two children, of course: Ronald, who was now 28 and running the business, and Lesley, doing her A levels at the local college.

Their house was the largest in the village of Highley, set in Shropshire on the west bank of the River Severn; detached with a double garage, built by George on land next to the business and still sharing the same telephone exchange with the business. George was always careful with his money and there was nothing ostentatious about the house or the man.

He would have been horrified at the litigation that followed his death when his wife Selina, whom he'd never divorced, surfaced to claim proper maintenance from his estate when she discovered his true wealth. After all, she argued, £2 a week was not a lot to live on, and the judge agreed. The case had been carefully followed in the local and national press, which set out who'd inherited what in the Whittle family.

Dorothy Whittle now reached the house and as usual drove straight into the open garage. She closed it up and entered the house through the front door, turning off the outside and garage lights. She made herself a hot drink, took a sleeping pill and, turning off the downstairs lights, made her way upstairs.

On her way to her room she looked in on Lesley, who was fast asleep in bed. Lesley had college next morning and would have spent the evening catching up with coursework and making a few phone calls. She always looked angelic as she lay there. Dorothy thought of Lesley as her best friend as well as her daughter. She smiled at the scene she'd seen a hundred times: Lesley asleep in bed with her dirty clothes thrown on the floor and next day's clothes folded neatly on the chair.

Finally Mrs Whittle reached her own room, undressed and, too tired to read, turned out the light and went straight to sleep.

Next morning she was up at 6.45 a.m. to take a pill for a headache and then went back to bed until 7.30 a.m., when she went downstairs to make Lesley's breakfast of coffee and cereal. She went into the lounge to open the curtains, but it wasn't very light yet and she noticed nothing unusual.

As usual she took up a bowl of cornflakes for Lesley to have in bed before she dressed for college. But this morning the bed was empty, so she assumed Lesley was in the bathroom. When she found the bathroom empty she called out to tell Lesley that breakfast was ready, but there was no answer from upstairs. She looked again in Lesley's room and this time noticed her clean clothes for the new day still lying on her chair, which made it unlikely that she'd left the house for a walk.

Now concern was turning to panic, and she checked downstairs, but all she could find was a box of Turkish delight sitting on a vase in front of the fireplace, with a coil of tape on top that she assumed must be something to do with Lesley's college work. She was too agitated to look any further.

There was nothing for it now but to telephone her son, Ronald. He lived at the other end of the village with his wife Gaynor and they'd know what to do. But the phone was dead. This was not particularly strange as the phone was still connected to the office and sometimes the girl on the exchange left the line open so you couldn't get a line from the house. Undaunted, Mrs Whittle went out to the car in her dressing gown and drove the mile to Ronald's, keeping an eye open the whole way for Lesley in case she really had gone for a walk in the village.

At Ronald's she found herself becoming incoherent, mainly because there was so little to say except that Lesley wasn't in the house. 'Lesley's not there,' she said helplessly. Ronald came downstairs. He wasn't really worried – there were several plausible explanations as to where she might be. 'Have you searched the house?' he asked.

Dorothy said she thought she had.

'She might have caught an earlier bus,' Ronald suggested.

'She can't have. All her clothes are there except her dressing gown,' said Dorothy.

Ronald was still sure there was an explanation. He went to the house and made a double-check, and then to the office to attend a training board meeting, but he was unable to concentrate and started phoning round to see if anyone had seen her.

At 9.45 a.m. Gaynor rushed down to the office. 'They've taken Lesley!' she cried, and showed Ronald the DYMO tape. Gaynor had made her own search of the house, only stopping when she came to something rather odd in front of the hearth in the lounge. It was the tall vase placed on the floor in front of the hearth with a box of Turkish delight perched on the top. On the box was a long coil of tape, the sort of thing you printed out and stuck on the front of files or cabinet drawers, which turned out to be four coils of tape when she picked them up.

It took a little time to read the DYMO tape on to which a long message had been laboriously printed, part of it in a sort of shorthand, parts with more detailed instructions. By the end of it Gaynor's hands were shaking. The essence of the message was a demand for a ransom of £50,000 in used notes, without any tricks or telling the police, otherwise it would be death, all couched in the stark language of an old-fashioned telegram:

```
NO POLICE £50.000 RANSOM BE READY
TO DELIVER FIRST EVENING WAIT FOR
TELEPHONE CALL AT SWAN SHOPPING
CENTRE TELEPHONE BOX 64711 64611
63111 6PM TO 1AM IF NO CALL
RETURN FOLLOWING EVENING WHEN
YOU ANSWER CALL GIVE YOUR NAME
ONLY AND LISTEN YOU MUST FOLLOW
INSTRUCTIONS WITHOUT ARGUMENT
FROM THE TIME YOU ANSWER THE
TELPHONE YOU ARE ON A TIME LIMIT
IF POLICE OR TRICKS DEATH
```

A second strip of tape said:

```
£50.000 ALL IN USED NOTES £25.000
£1 £25.000 £5 THERE WILL BE NO
EXCHANGE ONLY AFTER £50.000
HAS BEEN CLEARED WILL VICTIM BE
RELEASED
```

The third strip demanded:

```
DELIVER £50.000 IN WHITE SUITCASE
```

The fourth tape came as an afterthought:

```
SWAN SHOPPING CENTRE
KIDDERMINSTER
```

The bizarre way in which this was all presented, the coils of DYMO tape and the box of Turkish delight perched on a vase in front of the fire, had the air of a bad joke or student prank.

Without a word about the tape to Dorothy, Gaynor went straight to tell Ronald.

2

Donald Neilson sat at his desk 55 miles away at home in Bradford. He was at his debriefing as part of 'the plan'.

Approaching 40 he looked a lot younger, with an almost boyish complexion and a straightforward haircut that his mum might have given him, a hundred miles from the fashionable long hair of the seventies. He wore a denim camouflage jacket that he'd swapped for the dark anorak he'd worn on the operation, waterproof trousers and thick army surplus boots. His boots were muddy and he couldn't work out why – he must have walked through a flowerbed on his way into the house. On the desk was his tool bag, holding a black hood with two eye slits, a cartridge belt, a sawn-off shotgun and a hurricane torch. Also on the desk were maps, notepads with lists and messages to himself, an assortment of stationery and a Thermos flask of coffee from which he poured himself a cup, pleased to see that the coffee was still hot.

The operation had gone well. The target had been removed from the house in Highley in the early hours and taken to the hiding place without much protest from her. He'd been a bit worried that the girl wouldn't be up to getting down the drainage shaft at Kidsgrove. Getting her down the various ladders and through the water had been difficult, but she was a fit girl and the worst that had happened was her dressing gown getting wet. At one stage he'd even tried carrying her along the tunnel – she hadn't weighed much but the roof was too low and he kept hitting his head. He wondered how long it would take to dry down there, but at least she was warm in the sleeping bag and there were extra blankets if she needed one.

In front of him on the floor and draped over a couple of chairs was an assortment of old sleeping bags, blankets, pieces of rope and wire, a couple of kitbags covered in mud, boots, camping equipment (including a single ring stove and gas bottles) and another cartridge belt. Beyond them was an open wardrobe with a variety of clothes falling off hangers or simply stuffed into corners of the wardrobe, spilling out like the intestines of fresh carrion, again mostly military stuff, creased and in need of a wash. But ask him where any particular item was in this confusion and he could lead you straight to it. Not that anyone had ever asked for anything in here for the simple reason that no one was ever allowed in, not even his wife or daughter.

His wife Irene lay asleep in their bedroom over the landing from his office. In her bedroom, asleep on the floor below, was Kathryn, their 16-year-old daughter – just a year younger than the girl he'd kidnapped and still at school. He wondered for a second whether his victim was asleep in her sleeping bag on the foam mattress in her new home. He'd tried to think of everything she'd need for her stay. He'd already heated her up some chicken soup and left it for her in a Thermos – nice and hot, that was, nearly boiling. But she'd need something to help her pass the time. He'd get her some magazines, something a bit posh like *Vogue* because she came from a good background, certainly good enough to pay up a ransom without noticing too much. He could have asked for much more but they wouldn't notice £50,000. The last kidnapping he'd read about they were asking a million – stupid sum to ask for because no one could afford that. Perhaps some books as well as magazines if she was a college girl.

The page from the *Daily Express* that had inspired him to carry out the kidnapping still hung pinned to the wall behind him. It was page four of the issue dated Wednesday, 17 May 1975 and headlined, 'The Wealthy Man's £2 Wife – £106,000 Will Shock for Woman Who Lived Cheek by Jowl with Poverty for 30 Years.'

That woman was Mrs Selina Whittle who, after thirty years separated from George Whittle and never receiving more than £2 a week maintenance from him because he said he couldn't afford any more, discovered on his death that he was worth a small fortune. Most of it was in trust to Dorothy, his former secretary with whom he'd lived but never married, and their children, Ronald and Lesley.

Dorothy, the paper said, had come into George's life as a 25-year-old blonde he met on the bus. Eventually they lived together and she changed her name to Whittle, and they had a son and a daughter. To soften the blow of death duties, George settled the bulk of his estate on his son, who took over the business, and £82,500 to his daughter in a trust. He left the house and two other properties, bringing in a decent income, to Dorothy. But to Selina, from whom George had separated after fifteen years of marriage, he left nothing, although Ronald had offered to keep the £2 a week going. Selina was now 71, and on her own in Coventry living on £8 a week widow's pension and £1.55 supplementary benefit. 'Cheek by jowl with poverty' was how the judge described her situation, and awarded her £1,500 a year, payable out of the estate and backdated to her husband's death two years ago. 'It will not give her the kind of life she would have enjoyed had she remained married,' said the judge, 'but at least it will put her safely out of the danger of poverty.'

Selina Whittle said after the hearing, 'I shall look forward to a holiday when the money comes through.'

When Donald Neilson read the report he was incensed. It just wasn't fair. That poor woman had had to live in poverty while the estranged husband piled up the money from the business he'd probably set up with her help. The Neilson family had to live in near poverty while these immigrants came in and took all the good jobs or got state benefits while he had to resort to crime to get any sort of income. Where was the justice in that? It made his blood boil. Suppose he took one of the Whittles on holiday and asked for a slice of the cake to get them back? That would be fair, wouldn't it? Then perhaps he could take *his* family on holiday.

His takings showed only £11,000 for the last year after three post office raids and three postmasters dead. He once clocked it up in his head that he must have done at least 400 other burglaries in his time and with so little to show for it. So far he hadn't been caught, but luck wouldn't stay with him forever. What he needed now was the Big One, the jackpot, the one-off payday where he could start to relax and enjoy life a little.

That was another thing – the house. Grangefield Avenue was marooned on a traffic island with mostly immigrants as neighbours. They wouldn't give you the time of day, and while he sweated away at his carpentry doing odd jobs and building wooden sheds in the back garden to sell, those people seemed to get proper jobs without any trouble.

Donald poured himself another coffee. He felt better after a little rant and he must remember this was his special day, the day for which he'd been planning and preparing for three years. That's why everything was going to work perfectly, from the pickup, the ransom demand and then the drop. This was the man whom they failed after ten weeks' basic training on national service now showing them how to do it – the police, the poshos in Highley with the money, and his own family who sometimes didn't think him up to the mark.

He'd already shown – and this was something he'd probably proved in the exercise last night – that he was up to SAS standard, no trouble at all. In different circumstances they would welcome him. On his CV would be the stark truth that he could break into a house through the garage, get upstairs in the dark, wake and remove a 17-year-old girl from her bed and escort her out of the house without waking her mother sleeping in a room across the corridor.

He'd found where Highley was on the map and driven down to Shropshire one day for a little reconnaissance. He found the house – not very difficult in a small village. It was ideal for a raid and met all his requirements for a target: detached house, on a main road so that if anyone heard anything they'd put it down to traffic, and near a motorway so he could move around the country quickly. Usually he preferred not to use a car and rely on public transport, much safer that way as the police would be looking for a vehicle. But he'd need a car for a kidnap, and the house in Highley gave plenty of cover, with a side road and an estate at the back where he could park on his recce trips. He was also encouraged to see an integral garage which he'd be able to enter through a side door and from there into the house.

In further visits he worked out exactly who was living in the house – Mrs Whittle and her daughter. He'd even worked out who occupied which bedroom, and their various social habits, which evenings they went out and what sort of time they came home.

He had prepared himself for the eventuality of the victim screaming, the rest of the house waking and the exercise having to be aborted. He would have shot anyone in the house if necessary and that would be the end of it – the same way he'd dealt with the post office people when they'd tried their tricks. Dead men don't talk, nor dead women, and that was the simple truth. The whole thing was as daring as it was successfully executed. He who dares wins …

He'd taken enormous care in planning the operation, but finding where he was going to keep the prisoner while he awaited the ransom drop had been a piece of luck. The first idea had been to keep her in one of the lock-up garages he had dotted around the Midlands, but that posed problems in their proximity to other housing and garages. Then there was the question of the drop-off area. This, if anything, was more difficult. It had to be somewhere from which he could escape with the money even if he was being watched by the police. One possibility was beside a train track where the money could be thrown out of a carriage window, somewhere in the open where he could see anyone trying to follow him.

The next possibility was Dudley Zoo, with its high walls and a maze of caves and tunnels through which he could escape after the money was thrown or pulled over the wall in a bag. No one could see him and by the time they got across the wall he would be long gone. In fact, he'd found a passage from one of the caves that led, after a few hundred yards, into a street where he could park his car for the getaway. It was perfect – at times the passage reduced to just a few feet wide where he could soon take care of anyone trying to follow him with a single blast of his gun.

It was as he was following the railway line past Bathpool Park in Kidsgrove that he came upon a manhole cover that had been left partly open. He pulled the cover aside to see a ladder going down into the dark, and came back later with a torch to explore the labyrinth of tunnels underneath. It turned out to be a vast drainage system for the whole park, where some of the tunnels were wet with 6in of water running through them, while others were bone dry. And then, on a further and braver exploration, he found a ladder going down even deeper, with a narrow ledge or platform at the bottom of the tunnel less than 3ft wide. This must be some inspection platform for the bottom of the chamber where a stream ran 6ft or so below. It was reasonably dry, and so deep, at least 60ft below the surface, that any bug or tracking device left hidden with the money simply wouldn't work at that level.

And that's where the girl was now, safely installed on the metal platform in a sleeping bag, with her dressing gown hanging out to dry on the ladder, safe as houses until he'd got the money. The dressing gown would take a while to dry, and her slippers had got soaked wading through 6in of water, but she was tucked up in her sleeping bag so he shouldn't feel too bad about her. It was important no harm came to her because he needed her to get the instructions to the family about where to take the money.

He suddenly leant forward and grabbed the black hood, which he pulled over his head and arranged the slits over his eyes. Then he walked over to the mirror on the wall and looked at himself. He was surprised that wearing the hood and pointing a shotgun at them at point-blank range didn't mean people did what he told them to do. Those idiot postmasters who jumped him and tried to grab the gun had had to be dealt with. That was their fault and he had no conscience about their deaths. He only took a gun to keep control of the situation, and the only time he ever intended to use it was to give a warning shot – but, oh no, they had to try the heroics. And for what – a couple of thousand quid?

He fetched the gun from the desk and returned to the mirror, poking the stubby, sawn-off barrels in front of him and chattering away in his pidgin West Indian English to disguise his voice. His accent was rather good – after all, he'd heard it enough times from his neighbours, 'Give me keys, man. Keys and no tricks.'

Even when they did what they were told and he was tying them up, they still appeared more worried about themselves than even the money. One of the postmasters' wives had said she had arthritis and not to do the rope up too tight, if he didn't mind.

Donald removed the hood, put down the gun and saluted to himself in the mirror. 'Carry on, Neilson,' he said.

'Very good, sir,' he replied, saluted again and did a smart about-turn.

Now it was time to put the next part of the plan into action …

3

Lesley Whittle lay naked in a sleeping bag 60ft underground on a narrow metal platform at the bottom of a drainage shaft. It had taken them some time to climb down through a hatch and several ladders and passages, sometimes in the dry and sometimes through several inches of icy cold water. The hooded creature who'd ordered her out of bed at the house didn't say much, and when he did it was in a funny accent, making him hard to understand.

He'd come into her bedroom in the dark and shone a light in her face. He said, 'Don't make any noise. I want money.' She saw he had a gun, a double-barrelled shotgun with short barrels. He waved at her to get out of bed, and when he saw she hadn't any clothes told her to put some on, and all she could think of doing to be quickest was put on her blue dressing gown and her mother's slippers that she'd borrowed.

Then he motioned her to go out into the corridor, but as they did so they heard a noise coming from her mother's room at the end. He did a lot of pointing and grunting and when they finally got out of the room he told her to go downstairs. They went out of the house through the inside door into the garage, where she could see he'd taken the handle off the inside of the door and put it on the floor, and then outside through the garage door. When they were outside in the garden, she felt cold and shivered.

'Where the money?' he asked in that silly squeaky voice.

'In the bathroom,' she said.

'How much?'

'£200, in coins,' she replied, and hoped he might go back and get it and leave her alone. It was the money they kept at the end of the day from the office and they didn't think it was worth them taking that amount to the bank and then having to go back in the morning and get it all out again. She wondered how he knew there was money in the house in the first place.

But he didn't leave her alone and instead put tape around her mouth and then over her eyes and did the same around her wrists. He wasn't rough, but he was strong and she knew she couldn't stop him, even if she'd tried. Then he put her in the back seat of a car that must have been parked near the garden because it didn't take him long to lead her there and shut and lock the door.

The man wasn't very long; in minutes he was back and shoved something that felt like a couple of foam mats over her before driving off. In fact, she wondered if he'd forgotten about her because if he had found the money he wouldn't need her any more – £200 in cash was a lot of money and that should have kept him happy. It was always kept in the bathroom. She'd never thought of helping herself to it or borrowing from it – why should she? She only needed some cash for the bus to get to college and then something for lunch. Her clothes were just her jeans and a T-shirt and her Afghan coat in winter – hardly the high life – so that even her allowance of just over £20 a month often left money over. The only luxury she really looked forward to was having her own car and she was learning to drive now.

She never really thought about money. Even her jewellery, a lot of which she was still wearing because she went to bed in it, was made by her boyfriend. It was true she was going to come into some money her dad had left her, but that was all tied up until she was older and she'd decided she'd probably use it one day to buy a house. But there was no cash, except the £200 in the bathroom. Anyway, the figures mentioned in the newspapers when the whole thing blew up about how much her father had left was a big exaggeration and twice as much as the real figure in her case.

It crossed her mind that the man in the hood had read this and thought they were all very rich. She never bought anything very expensive; even the make-up she bought was influenced by whatever two-for-one bargains were going in the shops more than anything else. She had wanted a bookcase in her room and Ronald made one for her and had brought it around at the weekend. In fact, he'd just phoned up about it today – or was it yesterday now – and he was about the last person she'd spoken to before she went to bed. He'd asked her if it was all right and she'd thanked him and said it was fine.

She wished he was here now. He'd sort all this out.

Then she started struggling again and trying to shout through the tape stuck around her mouth. He must have heard her trying to shout and banging around because she heard the car stop. Suddenly he was pulling the covers off her and telling her to keep still. He tore the tape off her mouth and asked what she wanted. 'I want to go home,' she shouted at him.

'Be quiet,' he said. 'You've been kidnapped. Be quiet and you'll be all right. But if you not quiet I put you in boot.'

'I'll be quiet,' she said.

'Are you warm enough?' he asked, more kindly.

She nodded, and he said he'd check the heater was on. Then he taped her up again and she lay there until they stopped after what felt like hours, but was probably less than two hours. This time he led her from the car up a hill to somewhere cold on her feet. Then they stopped and the man said to wait here until he took a few things down. He said again not to move because she was being watched and she'd be in for it if she tried any tricks. She couldn't see anything anyway, so it wasn't much use. She heard the man pull back something metallic like a lid and climb down.

The man came back and he guided her through an opening on to a ladder where he told her to hang on while he threw her over his shoulder in a fireman's lift and carried her down the ladder, followed by another tunnel that you could nearly stand in. Then it was a walk into a tunnel with icy cold water where her slippers got soaked. He tried to carry her to stop her getting wet but he kept slipping so she said she'd walk. This was followed by a dry tunnel and another ladder, not so long this time, until they reached a narrow platform where he told her to wait while he brought down some more things. He took the tape off her eyes and unbound her hands. Then she could see he'd laid out a sleeping bag and a foam strip on the platform like a little bed.

The bottom of her dressing gown was soaking wet where it had dipped into the water and he told her to take it off to dry. She turned her back on him the best she could but there wasn't much room and she handed him the dressing gown, which he hung on the ladder and told her to get into the sleeping bag where it was a bit warmer. When he told her to get into the sleeping bag she thought he was going to get in with her and rape her. But he didn't and went on fussing with all the bits and pieces he seemed to have prepared for her on the ledge.

She wished she had her clothes, and could see them sitting on her chair at home ready for the morning. She wondered if her mother had woken up yet and guessed she hadn't because she could sleep through anything after her sleeping pills. Perhaps, thinking about it now, she should have screamed when he woke her up, but what would he have done then? And Mum would have woken up and got involved and that would only have upset her. Better it was this way and get it over.

He went through everything like a hotel manager pointing out what was provided for her comfort and how she'd be all right if she didn't do anything silly. Then he put a wire collar around her neck and did it up with a spanner. He said in his funny accent that he'd put something like tape around it to make it softer, and once he'd done that he relaxed a bit and made them some soup on a stove he set up on the landing above them and which he brought down in a flask. It was all a bit like camping with the sleeping bag and the wet and the cold. At points he'd stop and look around and say, 'It's okay, you get dry,' and feel the dressing gown hanging from a rung on the ladder.

She felt pleased and relieved that at one point he'd told her to take off the dressing gown and use it to dry her feet before she got into the sleeping bag. Standing there completely naked with her back to him nothing had happened, and if anything was going to happen surely it would have then?

She needed the soup and the attempt at conversation to stop her shaking. Her feet were the coldest because they'd had to slosh through freezing water on the way down. 'All ready for you,' he added and all the time he shone the torch on her. She could see he wasn't very tall in the way he curled up sitting in the corner.

'Could I have my dressing gown?' she asked. 'I don't think I'm going to be warm enough.'

'Dressing gown still wet,' he said. 'Blankets for you.' He reached to two blankets wrapped in plastic parcels and pulled one out of its wrapper and spread it over her.

'When can I go home?' she asked.

'When they pay money,' he replied, without explaining further.

'My mum will want me home.'

'Of course.'

'You will let me go home.'

'When they pay money,' he repeated.

The man then sat quite still for a few minutes without saying anything. Lesley couldn't see much of him, but she could hear his muttering occasionally, as if he was going through in his mind what he had to do. Finally he shone the torch down on his gloved hands in which he was now carrying a small portable tape recorder and a piece of paper. 'You read this. Message to your mother.'

The message, written in capital letters on lined paper, was quite legible in the torchlight. He placed the machine next to her, pressed a button clumsily with a gloved finger and told her to begin. She tried to read as strongly as possible so that she wouldn't worry her mother. At the end she even made a little joke about getting wet. 'There is nothing to worry about, Mum. I am okay. I got a bit wet but I am quite dry now. I am being treated very well, okay?'

She was quite pleased with that because she sounded well and strong, and the little bit about getting wet just might give them a clue to where she was. She thought he might object to this and get cross, but he didn't and just let her go on.

Another clumsy clunk on the button and the tape stopped. 'Good,' he said, and played it back to see it was all right. Then he was gone, up the ladder without a goodbye or explanation as to when he'd be back and what he was going to do. She was rather relieved he'd gone – it wasn't so much what he'd done in dragging her out of bed and driving her all this way to sit somewhere in the cold and dark, but the lack of conversation, as if he didn't talk to people very much and lived like this, like an animal at the bottom of a hole.

Lesley did the only thing she could do – lay back in the sleeping bag and tried to keep warm and calm. She knew they'd pay him anything he asked and so it wouldn't be long before she was out and back home. The only thing that worried her was being dumped in the middle of the countryside in a wet dressing gown and bare feet.

Perhaps it wasn't a sewer; it didn't smell much except of damp and now all was quiet she could hear water running underneath her. She put on the torch he'd left her and leant over to the edge of the platform and shone the torch down. There, about 8ft below her, was a stream of running water. She couldn't see if it was clear or not because it was inky black.

She lay back in the sleeping bag and tried to think what they'd be doing at home. The one she worried about most was her mother. First of all Dad dying a few years ago, and now this. She'd have told Ron and Gaynor at once, of course. Lesley hoped they wouldn't tell the police and just give him the money and make it quick. The police might catch him handing over the money and then he might not tell them where she was if he wasn't going to get any money.

What was the time? She didn't wear a watch in bed and so she wasn't wearing one now. All she had on was a silver band around her neck, now under the metal noose, her earrings and a few bangles on her wrist. They'd miss her at college. She was supposed to be handing in some maths homework this morning and she hoped they wouldn't think she hadn't come to college because she hadn't done the work. Ron would probably phone them and say she was sick and hoped to be back soon – it wouldn't surprise her if he didn't mention what had really happened at all in case it worried everyone. They might even think it was a scheme for raising money for charity – she'd forgotten to ask the man how much he was asking for her – £1,000? £10,000? A million?

Whatever it was, they'd pay it. But suppose it was a million – what did they do then? What happened if you hadn't got what they asked? Perhaps that's when you called the police.

4

Detective Chief Superintendent Robert Booth, CID chief of West Mercia Police, had received a phone call telling him about the kidnapping and decided he should take a look himself. He was already heavily involved in a murder case, but kidnap was so rare that it needed him to be involved. His own record in solving murders was 100 per cent, and his police force generally had a crime-solving rate at about twice the average for the country – but kidnap, now that was something else.

When he arrived at the Whittle household in Highley there were one or two cars in the driveway, but none of them marked to suggest police activity. He'd asked that police officers be in plain clothes and that the whole operation be kept low-key for the moment. Certainly there was nothing to suggest he was a policeman as he plodded his way from the car to the front door, looking more like a bank manager or perhaps the firm's accountant in his beige coat and scarf tied in a neat knot at the neck.

Inside the house there were one or two of his officers searching the rooms and taking fingerprints, and in the dining room a distraught

Mrs Whittle being comforted by her daughter-in-law, Gaynor, with a woman police officer. He was shown where the intruder had come in through a door from the garage into the lounge and made his way up the stairs, something made pretty obvious by the trail of mud over the carpets. He had a quick look upstairs at Lesley's bedroom where the clothes thrown on the floor were apparently her doing – no sign of a struggle – and then back downstairs to confirm there was little in the way of a forced entry, just a few screws taken out of the handle of the door into the lounge, and the outside door to the garage unlocked. Oh, and the telephone wires to the house had been cut.

Finally Booth was presented with the coils of DYMO tape sitting on top of the box of Turkish delight. He read through the longest of the four coils a couple of times:

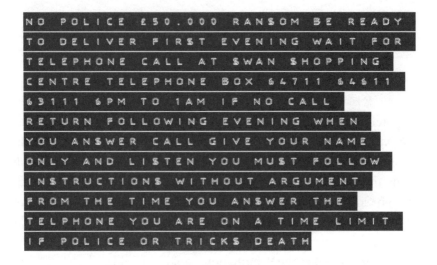

```
NO POLICE £50.000 RANSOM BE READY
TO DELIVER FIRST EVENING WAIT FOR
TELEPHONE CALL AT SWAN SHOPPING
CENTRE TELEPHONE BOX 64711 64611
63111 6PM TO 1AM IF NO CALL
RETURN FOLLOWING EVENING WHEN
YOU ANSWER CALL GIVE YOUR NAME
ONLY AND LISTEN YOU MUST FOLLOW
INSTRUCTIONS WITHOUT ARGUMENT
FROM THE TIME YOU ANSWER THE
TELPHONE YOU ARE ON A TIME LIMIT
IF POLICE OR TRICKS DEATH
```

This was followed by the shorter tapes that set out how the money was to be made up and delivered, and finally the tape confirming that it was the Swan Shopping Centre in Kidderminster.

Booth frowned. 'I'm not happy with these,' he said to one of his officers.

'Bad business, sir, and a young girl.'

'No, I meant it's all too amateur. He doesn't mention the girl, he doesn't say who's to deliver the money, and the ransom itself is ridiculously low. I mean, why pick on these people? – Highley isn't exactly Hollywood.

Whoever it is looks like he got the idea last night, grabbed the girl and is probably thinking this morning he's made a big mistake.'

'I see what you mean, sir,' said the young officer, impressed with the swift diagnosis.

'The girl's a student, isn't she?'

'Doing her A Levels at college, sir.'

'Then what's to tell us this isn't all some sort of student stunt? Check with the college and see if anything's going on there. Is there a boyfriend?'

'I believe there is; Mrs Whittle was saying something about a steady boyfriend.'

'Okay, same goes for him. See if there's been any big row lately and whether he's likely to pull something like this. I'll have a word with the mother.'

Booth took a deep breath before he made his way into the dining room. He had children of his own and could imagine what a mother was going through. Then he decided he couldn't imagine it, and went in anyway.

Mrs Whittle was sitting at the dining room table in front of an untouched cup of coffee. Gaynor sat next to her. Booth parked himself in front of them and explained who he was.

'I'm sorry we aren't seeing you in the lounge, but I can't face it knowing he's been in there,' said Mrs Whittle. Gaynor tactfully asked him if he'd like a cup of coffee and left the room.

'Mrs Whittle, you'll forgive me having to ask a few questions about Lesley. The first one, and probably least tactful at this stage, is would Lesley do this sort of thing as a joke?'

Dorothy Whittle straightened in her seat, taken by surprise. 'A joke? Oh no, she wouldn't do anything like this. She's a sensible and serious girl. We're very close, you know, and she wouldn't put us through all this.'

'Not a college jape, if that's the word, to collect money?'

'Not £50,000,' she replied, taking him literally.

'Is there anything to suggest to a kidnapper you might have this sort of money?'

Mrs Whittle stirred the cold cup of coffee she wasn't going to drink. 'Well, all I can think of is that since George's death there's been a rather unfortunate court case where his wife asked for more maintenance. All the family finances have been aired and the accounts in the newspapers make us sound very rich – although we aren't because it's tied up in trusts, you see. Lesley's share is in a trust and she can't touch that until she's at least 25.'

'So someone could have read about all this and got the wrong conclusion?'

'Don't think we won't pay it. We'll pay anything they ask to get her back, of course.'

'That's something else that makes me a little suspicious, Mrs Whittle. £50,000 in the general scheme of things isn't a lot to ask in a kidnapping. They usually ask for a lot more.'

Gaynor brought in the coffee and at the same time one of the officers poked his head around the door. Booth went out into the hall. 'We've finished the search, sir. Nothing missing, except for some jewellery and a dressing gown and slippers the girl was wearing when she was taken. There was two hundred quid in cash in the bathroom but that wasn't touched. Looks like he only went into the girl's room upstairs and then came straight down with her.'

Booth went back into the dining room and Gaynor offered again to leave. 'No need to leave us – there's only one more thing I'd like to put to you, Mrs Whittle. How does an intruder like this get up the stairs in the middle of the night, go into your daughter's bedroom and wake her up, take her downstairs and out through the garage – all this without waking you?'

Dorothy Whittle found this difficult to answer. She shook her head as if this was a question she'd already asked herself a dozen times. 'I think I can answer that,' said Gaynor, watching her mother-in-law reduced nearly to tears again. 'The truth is that once Dorothy has taken her sleeping pill she's dead to the world. She wouldn't have heard a thing.'

Dorothy nodded. Gaynor shook her head.

By now Booth was sufficiently convinced that the kidnap was genuine and spent the afternoon putting plans into place to snare the kidnapper or any accomplice should he choose to collect the money personally from Ronald that evening, rather than leave further directions for a pickup or delivery through a phone call, and by 6 o'clock everything was in place. Ronald carried two cases of bank notes to the telephone boxes – two because the amount of money wouldn't fit into one case, despite the request in the ransom message – and started his wait. Plain-clothes officers infiltrated the area, some on the ground, some in surrounding offices, one even in the back of Ronald's car carrying a gun.

A pretence was also kept up that there was no connection between Ronald and the police. During the afternoon, a local freelance Kidderminster journalist living next door to the Whittle office got wind of the kidnap and that the police operation was set up at the Swan Shopping Centre. He telephoned the police station at about the same time that Ronald started his wait, but was told neither one thing nor the other. There was no confirmation, nor was there a denial, just that they'd been told not to say anything. The journalist told a local newspaper and then at 7.30 p.m. told BBC television. The BBC themselves then rang Kidderminster to be met with the same blank wall, and the story went out as a newsflash.

The news was out. Booth was horrified. Working on the assumption that no one was going to find out about the kidnapping or the police operation, at least not this quickly, he had to think what to do, and called a hurried news conference to confirm that Lesley Whittle had indeed been kidnapped and described what she was wearing. The conference was packed with journalists and one of them told Booth that one of the regional newspapers had then found out the location of the telephone boxes and added that to the copy.

The assumption was now that with news bulletins going out every hour the kidnapper would be frightened away. Members of the public were starting to assemble in the shopping centre to watch the drama for themselves rather than on television. By 9 p.m., with the whole possibility of secrecy blown sky high, both the police and Ronald Whittle were ordered back to the police station to think what to do next while Booth went to his press conference.

At the police station the most senior officers in the investigation decided to have their own meeting and sent everyone else home, including Ronald who drove back to Highley from Kidderminster with two armed detectives. Members of the press went off to file their stories for the following day's newspapers, and then collected in the bars of local hotels to see what tomorrow brought. Booth had made it clear, like a headmaster berating his prefects, that he was 'disappointed' that the story had been leaked and reported. Well, he only had to ask, was the general response from journalists, and we would have held the story.

As senior officers sat into the night discussing how to play it the next day, and the gentlemen of the press nursed their pints in the bar, the stage in the Swan Shopping Centre that had earlier been the centre of so much planning and concealed activity was now empty, the players and their uninvited audience gone for the night. Only the props remained, three empty telephone boxes that, as midnight struck, suddenly sprung into life and starting ringing, one by one, to an empty theatre.

5

Donald Neilson woke up on the following morning about as furious as Detective Chief Superintendent Booth, but for very different reasons. While Booth saw his plans made on the trot over twenty-four hours dramatically fall apart as the previous evening had worn on, Neilson's preparation for the kidnap had taken him three years of meticulous planning: how and where to seize the victim, where to take and hide the victim, how the ransom would be handed over and last, but certainly not least, how or whether to return the victim once the money was handed over without his, Neilson's, identity being discovered.

Then, after all this, he telephones as arranged on the night and no one answers. Or to be precise, someone does pick up on the third call who is obviously nothing to do with the Whittle family. Don't they care he's got their daughter lying naked at the bottom of a drainage shaft praying someone will get the money together and be at the end of a phone to get directions for where to take it? He'd even told them the type of bag he wanted the money in and how the money was to be made up. He'd given them the choice of three telephone boxes in case they were being used by the public. He'd even anticipated this sort of disorganisation and said if they couldn't be bothered on the first evening then to try again on the next.

He knew they'd got the message because he'd left it there, on top of the Turkish delight, large as life. Perhaps he ought to pop in there again tonight and put the appointment in their diary and then they wouldn't forget, or send a taxi round at the appointed time, or both.

So now it had to be another call tonight.

Most important, he'd told them no police. That's why he hadn't rung until midnight, just to give himself the chance to check for himself the police weren't lurking. Satisfied they weren't, he'd driven the 30 miles back to Dudley and telephoned from a telephone box there, only to find that not only were there no police but no family either.

Now, of course, everybody knew: it was plastered all over the morning papers and on the television. Last night he hadn't heard the early bulletins on local radio and then television simply because he wasn't at home, too busy checking everything for the telephone call. But for the moment he'd leave things as they were and assume they'd be there to answer his call tonight.

For three days he'd been camping in the car. It was January and it was cold, and while it was okay when he was driving with the heater on – and there'd been a lot of driving what with getting the girl up to Kidsgrove from Highley and then driving back down to Dudley to arrange the drop – he couldn't use the heater while the car was parked and the nights were cold. He had a sleeping bag in the back of the car but it was cold by morning, and he hadn't had a decent shave or wash. He felt like a bloody tramp and looked like one when he saw himself in a shop window. Still, that was what he was trained for and his reward would come, but it hadn't helped his temper when no one turned up to answer the phone.

Today had been spent rechecking the various messages he'd left in telephone boxes for Ronald Whittle, assuming it would be him now he had the girl. The plan was to collect and follow the messages through to the wall at Dudley Zoo, where the bag of money would be tied to a rope and hauled over the wall. If they'd answered the phone last night then it would be all over by now.

The thing that was worrying Neilson most was someone using one of the telephones today, finding a message and breaking the link. He'd meticulously printed them on a series of DYMO tapes and then stuck them either behind the telephone board in each box or underneath the shelf covering the telephone directories. He made sure that each message was well out of sight so no one would find it by mistake. Meanwhile, he'd be able to check from a distance that no one was trailing him as Whittle made his way around the boxes. It was foolproof, he thought, a plan dreamt up over a long time and tested.

Foolproof – that was the word. These fools had already shown they couldn't wait at a phone box for a call that was going to bring them back the girl.

Now he'd reached the Freightliner depot in Dudley where Whittle was going to be directed to a message stuck to one of the lamp posts, and from there to one of the gates at the zoo over the road. Neilson had parked the car and was walking through the car park outside the depot towards the lamp post, when he saw someone watching him from a distance. The man, whose name was Gerald Smith, was tall, bald, and at first Neilson thought he was a policeman, but then relaxed a little when the uniform looked more casual, nothing much more than a uniform jacket, one of the drivers, perhaps, of one of the lorries left in the car park. Still, he couldn't chance it and slid the .22 pistol he carried in his bag into his coat pocket just in case.

Neilson carried on into the car park and hovered behind one of the lorries. Still, the man came up after having a chat with a crane driver on the site, and Neilson now emerged from behind the lorry to avoid looking as if he was hiding. The two had to say something to each other, they were so close. Neilson assumed he was talking to one of the drivers coming back to his cab. He mumbled something about getting a lift to Jackson's warehouse, where he'd once had a job driving a forklift.

He could see now this was a Freightliner man, probably security, because he started asking Neilson why he wanted to go there, and all

Neilson could think of saying was that he'd find out when he got there. Now it was getting silly.

Without further ado the man turned on his heels and started walking briskly back to the depot. It was obvious he was going to tell the police and have him arrested. Neilson had to think quickly. All he could see was the whole operation falling apart at the seams. Neilson reached into his coat pocket and pulled out the revolver. He fired once at the man's bottom but he kept on running. The next shot was in his back, that should bring him down and Neilson could make a run for it.

But that didn't work either. The idiot came back at him, and started shouting at him and calling him names. He even had the gall to take a swing at him but missed. He was asking for it. This time Neilson fired four more shots at him at point-blank range, but even then the target started to run, like one of those horror films where as much as you pump shots into the alien it keeps on running.

Neilson ran on after him, until the target stumbled and he had him, on the ground and panting like someone who'd run a mile, looking straight up at him. From 6ft Neilson levelled the gun and pulled the trigger.

Nothing happened. Just a click. He was out of ammo. Now it was his turn to run, but once he'd reached the streets he slowed down to walking pace, remembering his training not to give himself away by looking like a fugitive. With luck the target wouldn't make it. He walked and walked, and in Tipton Street, just when he was getting his breath back, he saw a police car pass him and then stop 50 yards down the street.

This time he did run. He didn't care who saw him. He was near the hospital and slipped into a gate near the nurses' home rather than try to climb the wall around the hospital. Once inside the grounds of the home and out of sight, he stopped to catch his breath. But just as he was starting to congratulate himself, a terrible thought struck him. The car. It was parked only 100 yards or so from the shooting.

The police would find it and all the gear in there: the spare sleeping bag, the spare mattress, the tape of the girl giving directions, and the envelopes carefully marked with directions on the route to the drop. They'd know the man they were chasing was the Black Panther, the man who'd shot the security guard, who'd shot three postmasters, and who'd now kidnapped Lesley Whittle.

He stood with his back against the wall, still trying to get his breath, and wept with frustration. This was three years' work and he'd messed it up, just like he did everything else. It was his own bloody fault: why did he have to shoot the man? He could have told the truth and said he'd parked his car and was taking a short cut through to the zoo – what was wrong with that?

He started walking, quietly and unhurried, chin up. Behind him was the occasional wail of a police siren. They wouldn't have found the car yet but it wouldn't be long. There was a way through this. Just get the girl to make a new tape with a new drop. Make it nearer the girl instead of all this phone box business. Tonight was off now, of course.

One thing was for sure now. The police would tell Whittle all about the shooting and make him think twice about ever letting the police back into the picture. He knew now that if anything went wrong or if there was the slightest suspicion that the police were involved in the next drop then it was curtains for the girl. The Panther shot to kill. The police would keep out of it – they wouldn't want to risk her getting hurt. It was just … he hadn't got a car now to get back up to the girl, nor to drive her anywhere after a successful drop. But he could leave her where she was and leave a message somewhere for them to find her.

He was getting his breath back and lengthening his stride, swinging his arms like the soldier he was. In the SAS you didn't give up, you made another plan and didn't make a song and dance about it. Yes, he'd leave her there, on the platform at the bottom of the shaft. Now he thought about it he hadn't made any real plan what to do with her afterwards. Getting away with it was the important thing, even more important than the money.

6

The game of musical chairs for that evening of Wednesday, 15 ~~February,~~ the second day of the kidnap, ended at 1 a.m. for Ronald Whittle and his police team without any result. This time they had waited until 1 a.m. without a phone call, whereas on the previous evening they had given up at 9 p.m. and, unknown to them, missed the phone call at midnight.

On the blunder count it was two all: first the police not requesting a shut-down on all news getting into the media and then pulling out Ronald and the team early in the evening only to miss the call; followed by Donald Neilson himself making an unnecessary attack on Gerald Smith and abandoning his car crammed with information linking him to the kidnap.

Now, even at this late hour of the night, it was someone else's turn to try to mess up the investigation. In the early hours the telephone rang at the Whittle home in Highley and a man's voice demanded that the ransom money be taken to a subway in a park in Gloucester. The caller said that the money should be delivered within ninety minutes otherwise Lesley would be killed. The police were informed and as soon as the beleaguered Ronald got home from his abortive wait at the Kidderminster telephone boxes he had to set sail again with his police team.

There was a high expectation that this was the real thing after waiting so long at Kidderminster because it was quite likely that the kidnapper had been put off by all the publicity in the last twenty-four hours, and particularly by the presence of both the press and the public during the evening around the telephones in the Swan Shopping Centre. Determined that this time no news would be leaked of this development, the police set up a roadblock at the slip road on to the M5 that allowed Ronald and his escort through, but not the following posse of news journalists.

By 2.15 a.m. all was in place and Ronald sat in his car with the money near the Gloucester subway entrance. But in a familiar pattern that was becoming the hallmark of this case, nothing happened. No one came near the car and so eventually Ronald got out and walked alone to the subway with the money. He shouted out an invitation for whoever it was to come and collect the money and that he wasn't leaving it until he saw his sister. Still no response, and no one to be seen except for a couple walking the dog, and they took no notice and walked on by.

This time, it turned out, the call was a hoax. A couple living near the subway had seen all the publicity on the news and the Whittle phone number and devised their own plot to make some quick money. A telephone call was all it needed, and under the pretext of walking the dog the same couple seen by Ronald had walked around the area long enough not only to see Ronald sitting in the car, but a few furtive police officers crouching in the bushes ready to relieve them of the money and their freedom for a few years. After a police hunt the man had vanished, leaving the woman to receive a four-year prison sentence, missing her opportunity to emigrate to Australia with her four children.

This time the police presence at least made sure that Ronald wasn't going to lose his money without the return of his sister, but had this been the real thing with Neilson ready to carry out his part of the exchange, the assumption is that he wouldn't have had much trouble spotting the police presence and abandoning ship quickly. Ronald drove the trip home to Highley wondering for the first time whether this wasn't some sort of macabre joke after all: the abortive call last night, no one phoning at all tonight, and then making him trail all the way down to Gloucester for apparently no reason except to enjoy making him look a fool again. What sort of person was this with such a perverted sense of humour? The fact that the call had come at the end of an evening of waiting made it all the more authentic, as if there was a real reason why the kidnapper couldn't make the call to the telephone box. Perhaps he'd seen the police on both occasions, and this begged the question as to whether they could ever organise a handover now with a police presence.

For the first time Ronald seriously doubted whether they should ever have told the police; it all seemed to be endless delay with nothing at the end. He wanted to hand the money over as much as the kidnapper wanted to receive it, and the question of whether anyone was caught was frankly irrelevant at the moment as long as they got Lesley back.

At daylight the police continued routine searches of the area of the Gerald Smith shooting, including one surprise when the shutter of one of the lorries parked in the zoo car park rattled up and out jumped the driver after his night's sleep in the trailer. While he was able to show he was the driver, he was at a loss as to how he failed to hear the shooting when it was so close. But a bigger surprise came after finding three live and six used rounds of .22 ammunition. When these were examined by forensics the marks left by the firing-pins on the used cartridges revealed the startling news that the gun used to shoot Gerald Smith was the same as that used to kill two sub-postmasters at Accrington and Langley. The Black Panther, the man the police had been hunting over the past three years for three murders in three post office raids, was the one and same who'd just shot Gerald Smith.

The other routine search and check following the Smith shooting was of all cars parked within a mile of the scene, but computer checks showed none of the vehicles to have been stolen. This search included a dark green Morris 1100 parked only 150 yards away from the shooting scene in a car park across the road from the local bus station. The registration number TTV 454H did not tally with the tax disc on the windscreen, but no one noticed. The car, stolen by Neilson some months ago, had been parked there and left by him minutes before the shooting. It was the car used to take Lesley Whittle away from her home and was packed with tools and apparatus used by Neilson in the operation.

So the car remained there in the car park, untouched and gathering dust, with the police unaware of its significance, and Donald Neilson assuming the police would by now have found it and the treasure trove of tools, bedding and tapes that would have told the police in an instant that they could add Lesley Whittle's kidnap to their list of crimes committed by the Black Panther.

7

Lesley Whittle lay in her damp sleeping bag 60ft underground on a narrow metal platform. It was pitch dark in the drainage shaft and while she could have put on the lantern he'd left at the bottom of the steps, she was starting to worry when and if the man was going to come back.

For the first few hours she'd kept the lantern on, too frightened to turn it off and be in the dark, but she'd kept her head enough to realise the batteries wouldn't last forever and the thought of being stranded in the dark was more daunting. Anyway, it wasn't as if she was missing anything with the light on. She was kept company by the sound of running water underneath her, and the occasional scratching and splashing of what she guessed were rats. But at least it was the sound of life; that and the occasional rumble of a train through the walls of the shaft like a London tube train.

The only reminders she had of home were what she was wearing: her silver necklace with a pendant made by her boyfriend, silver earrings and silver ring on her right hand, and six silver bangles on her right wrist. Everything she'd been wearing when she was woken up and marched out of the house.

The dressing gown was still hanging from one of the rungs of the ladder in an attempt to dry but, like everything else down there, it was still damp. Her slippers were sodden after splashing through all that water on the way down. It was a bit like boarding school when suddenly you didn't have your bedroom or your mother around you any more. On her first night at school she'd told herself not to worry about seeing them all at home again and it was going to be the same this time.

Only now she was alone in the dark with a wire noose around her neck …

The question was, when was she going to see her family again? She thought at times she must have dozed off, but without daylight it was hard to tell. It wasn't so much waking up and wondering where she was, it was wondering if she was alive at all. She felt she was lying in a shroud in a padded coffin somewhere deep in the bowels of the earth, where she'd been buried for at least a day now with everyone gone home after the funeral.

They'd be talking about her, and she hoped they'd be saying nice things, but the man who'd brought her down here wouldn't be at the service or the party afterwards because – and she'd thought about this quite a lot while she'd been lying there – he might be Death itself. She'd only seen him in darkness, dark when he brought her here in the night, dark when he'd brought her down the tunnels. He wore dark clothes, he wore a dark hood. It sounded silly, but who else would want to bury her like this so suddenly and then leave her without food and water except for that salty soup? That must be Death, who takes you out of bed in the middle of the night, tapes you up so you can't even say goodbye to Mum, and then drives you in the back of his car to your grave, where he escorts you down into the earth and puts you in a shroud and coffin, and then disappears back up the ladder and leaves you there.

If he came back again she'd ask him who he was, even if he put another tape across her mouth. She'd ask him what the weather was like up there and how the ransom was coming on. She knew they would pay, even if it meant selling the house or Ron selling his car. Dad would have paid in the end, but he was more careful about his money and he might have tried to beat the sum down before he actually paid up. He would have given the Death man a right mouthful and told him to get a job to earn some money rather than take her away like this.

The other thing that worried her was that when the man let her go, where that would be, because she only had a dressing gown to wear, and that would be pretty embarrassing if it was in a village or by the motorway, or something like that. Maybe he could arrange for some of her clothes to be picked up from home and got out to her, like you did when you came out of hospital.

All this was assuming he'd come back at all. He might have other people to take down a hole and have to look after them too. She could hear water running in what sounded like a stream underneath her, but she couldn't risk going down there because the wire might not stretch and she'd be stuck and not able to get back up.

Then there was the question of whether Death man was a man at all. Under that black hood he might be hideously deformed. He might be the Hunchback of Notre Dame or the Elephant Man. His voice was odd, a bit squeaky and not using many words. Perhaps he didn't want a ransom at all. Perhaps he was just going to keep her there for his pleasure; perhaps he'd lost a dog and wanted to keep her instead on the end of a leash and bring her up at night to walk around outside, and then one night just let her loose, although that was rather unlikely after all the trouble he'd gone to in making that taped message to her mum about the money and the instructions.

Perhaps she'd been dreaming, because suddenly it was raining bits and pieces of muck on her face. She sat up and leaned over to the lantern to switch it on. They were pieces of dirt and flakes of rust falling on her, and she grabbed the polythene bag that had wrapped the blanket and threw it over her head. Now she could hear footsteps on the rungs of the ladder, and he was down, only he wasn't dressed as Death this time but as a human being, with wavy hair and eyes and mouth instead of a slit.

He didn't look very pleased, but perhaps he always looked that. She didn't know how he always looked. He seemed older than she imagined for someone who moved so quickly and agilely, but tired, with a thick stubble on his chin now she could see him more clearly in the light of the lantern, and he wore a cap and a coat, not the black things he wore last time. He wasn't deformed and she wondered why he wore a hood at all – perhaps he didn't want Mum or anyone to see his face when he came into the house in case they recognised him.

Neilson half sat and half slumped against the wall at the end of the platform, nearly sitting on Lesley's feet as he did so. He drew his knees up to his chin to avoid them pairing on the narrow platform like sardines in a tin. His eyes were bloodshot through lack of sleep and the stubble on his chin told her he hadn't shaved for days and, judging by the smell, hadn't washed either. For a moment Lesley wondered if this was the same man who'd brought her in in the first place. Perhaps it was a tramp who'd found his way in and just wanted some company.

Lesley half sat up in the sleeping bag, pulling the front of the bag up tight to her neck. She felt she had to speak to him as the only likely way to help herself. He was the one who'd brought her down here and he was the only one who was going to get her out. 'Have they given you the money?' she asked.

He sat there, his head on his knees, not saying a word.

'I'm a bit hungry and thirsty. Could I have something, please?' she tried again.

He looked up at her. His eyes were funny. Not just bloodshot, but as if he wasn't there, right in the back of his head. 'No time. Change of plan,' he said finally. He crashed one of his boots down on the metal platform, sending the report rolling around the tunnels like a gunshot. 'Food when we get money!' he shouted.

'Do you live here?' Lesley asked, aware it was a silly question but it was all she could think of saying, as if the hours alone in the dark had numbed her brain.

'Live in house, not here,' he replied. 'With money, buy better house.'

'I'd like to go back to my house,' said Lesley.

'When we get money.'

Lesley felt pleased that at least she'd been included in the plan. It was when *we* get the money, not just him. He'd have to keep her alive. She noticed that he'd brought a bag down with him, which he now unzipped and pulled out the tape recorder. He pulled out a scruffy piece of paper from his pocket and passed it to her. 'You read,' he said.

She cleared her throat as he pressed the record button with a grubby gloved finger. 'Mum, you are to go to Kidsgrove Post Office telephone box. The instructions are inside, behind the backboard. I'm okay. But there's to be no police and no tricks, okay?'

She was asked to repeat this twice. She surprised herself how calm and in control she sounded. He started to pack the tape recorder back into the bag. 'You haven't got anything to eat in there?' she asked.

He fished into the bag and pulled out the sawn-off shotgun. 'No police or tricks,' he said, pointing the barrel up the steps. He didn't pull the trigger or make any noise, simply stuffed the gun back into the bag and brought out a pistol, like a child showing a friend his toys. Then he started laughing; a low, mirthless laugh. 'This is what he got this afternoon,' he announced, barely able now to contain himself.

8

For Dorothy Whittle it had been days of agony, jumping every time the telephone rang, at night waking every hour to relive the nightmare. If it was the phone during the day then it was usually someone ringing to sympathise, but while appreciated by Dorothy all she could do was to ask them to clear the line in case the kidnapper called.

Each day piled on the agony as the question remained why the kidnapper didn't contact the family, even if it was just to say Lesley was safe. All daily routine had stopped now and Dorothy relied on a cleaner to come in the morning and on Gaynor to do the cooking. For the first night or two Dorothy got no sleep at all, but now at least she snatched a few hours.

She wondered how she had the strength to carry on. She was told they'd said prayers for Lesley at the local Church of England and Methodist churches in the village and that helped her. Like Ron, she wished that word about the kidnap hadn't got out so quickly and just given them the chance to hand the ransom over and get Lesley back – then they could do what they liked about reporting it in the newspapers and on television. The kidnapper might have been put off.

Who'd told the press and television? It wasn't the police, Mr Booth assured them of that. It must have leaked out in the village was the only way she could think of. You couldn't blame them, really, and all those cars at the front of the house in the drive must have told them something was going on.

Some friends had called in to see her every day and she blessed them for that, helping her get through the hours. She hadn't been out of the house herself at all, except for one trip at the end of the previous week to the magistrates' court at Bridgnorth when they caught a hoaxer who'd called her for a demand of £2,500 to return Lesley and the police had swiftly caught him – one of many hoaxers, unfortunately. Ron was saying now that it was getting so bad with people, cruel people, seizing the chance to make some quick money. It wasted so much time and the police were rushed off their feet in trying to interview people as it was.

Meanwhile, she couldn't watch television, and couldn't concentrate enough to read or look at the papers – all she had the strength to do was sit and wait with her marvellous friends from the village and pray that call came.

She'd been offered tranquillisers but she'd refused any medication like that because she wanted to keep a clear head for when the kidnapper called and she had to take down directions. She was experienced with that after all those years in the office having to take calls from customers about where they wanted a coach and where they wanted it taken to. She imagined that when the call came she'd be able to take the instructions in one go and not have to ask for them to be repeated. There was a writing pad and pen always ready by the phone.

At first when the police really thought the kidnap itself might be some sort of hoax she'd been adamant there was no way Lesley would ever do a thing like that. She was a serious girl, and daughter and mother were very close, she'd never put her mother through that. Any suggestion that she might be trying to get her inheritance early was complete nonsense. This figure of £82,500 in a trust was equally nonsense and had come up in that court case with George's wife – about half that figure was more like the truth, and Lesley wouldn't inherit that until she was 25.

There was certainly nothing showy about Lesley's way of life to justify all this talk about her being an 'heiress'. All she wanted now was to pass her three A levels at college and then go on to university and a teaching career. Dorothy gave her a modest allowance that paid her travel expenses and meals at college, and that was about it. She didn't have many friends in the village for the simple reason she'd either been away at boarding school or abroad in the holidays. Her college friends were scattered around the place and her boyfriend lived 20 miles away from Highley.

If anyone thought raising the ransom money of £50,000 had been easy, well, go and ask their bank manager. They'd had to mortgage the house and business to raise the money and it was probably just as well they'd known the manager for some time to be able to do that at short notice. Anyway, they had the cash now, in a large suitcase ready to take out when the call came and, as Ron put it, if that meant going to the South Pole then so be it if they got Lesley back. The suitcase was so heavy even Ron could hardly lift it.

How anyone had got into the house and removed Lesley was a mystery, not least because there was usually someone around from the village even in the early hours of the morning and they would have seen a car or a stranger snooping around. There'd been suggestions that it was an 'inside job' because the intruder seemed to be familiar with the layout of the house to break in and know where to find Lesley, but that seemed ridiculous. The Whittles were pillars of the village and well liked, and no one would expect a thing like this to happen.

The very idea that someone had been in the house gave her the creeps, mud up and down the stairs, fiddling around with messages and the vase in the lounge, into Lesley's bedroom and her asleep, the whole thought of it was horrible. The man obviously had no family of his own, because no one with a daughter could possibly do anything like that. If he did have a daughter then the only consolation might be that he was looking after Lesley now, making sure she wasn't too scared and feeding her properly and making sure she was warm and comfortable. It was only this thought that was keeping Dorothy going.

Still, and the thought would haunt Dorothy to her dying day, how did someone break into your house, come upstairs and remove your daughter from under your nose without you hearing? Thank God she had Ron, who was as calm and collected as usual; if they'd taken him and left her to do the negotiating and deliver the money, well, she'd be in a mental home by now.

She thought Mr Booth was probably quite grateful to have Ron as well. Poor Mr Booth seemed as worried as they were and as upset about the news getting out before they'd had time to negotiate, and then the next night no call coming at all and the hoax taking Ron gallivanting down to Gloucester. Mr Booth had seen nothing like it, even in his long service as a police officer. Murder was his trade, people said, and with that he'd been 100 per cent successful.

But kidnapping was different from murder – God forbid it came to that. And then, on the third evening, the call came.

9

Len Rudd, as manager of the Whittle's depot at Highley, knew Lesley as well as anyone in the firm. He'd known her since she was a baby and he'd seen her go through at least a couple of private schools where she wasn't particularly happy. But she was back from boarding school now and going to college, with a steady boyfriend, and things were working out for her. Even at boarding school, she would come into the office to work during the holidays. While not aloof or, as a member of the Whittle family, one to pull rank or expect to be treated differently, she kept herself to herself and expected to be paid for her work.

But the last couple of days had been very difficult for Len, trying to balance the tragedy facing the family with the necessity of keeping the company going without Ronald. Dorothy Whittle was spending most of the time at Gaynor's, asking Len to take calls coming into the Whittle home, including any night-time calls.

And so, by 11.45 that Thursday evening Len was already in bed when his phone rang. He was aware of the number of hoax calls that had come in and the strain it had put on Ronald and the family in having to dash around the country to one false rendezvous after another, until Ronald decided that he wouldn't pursue any of the calls unless he had definite proof that the call was genuine. The phone was down in the kitchen and it took Len seconds to get there. He picked up the receiver and immediately heard the pips that told him it was a telephone box. 'Hello, Highley 613,' he said. There was no answer. 'Hello, Whittles,' he said.

Then he heard Lesley's voice saying something about going to a telephone box in Kidsgrove. He tried to interrupt and ask her how she was and was everything okay, but she didn't seem to be able hear him, and then the message started again. 'Mum, you are to go to Kidsgrove Post Office telephone box. The instructions are inside, behind the backboard. I'm okay, but there's to be no police or tricks …'

He grabbed the pad and pencil he kept by the phone and started writing furiously, desperate not to miss the slightest detail. There was no tremor or uncertainty, just a calm voice giving a set of instructions without a hint of fear or hysteria. While Lesley kept talking Len would interrupt to ask, 'Hello, Lesley, where's that again, where's that again?', but with no change in inflection the voice was obviously a tape recording.

But there was another voice there besides Lesley's, a shrill, high-pitched whistling sound in the background when she stopped talking that was definitely not electrical interference. But it was impossible to tell if it was male or female. Len thought it was from while the tape was being made rather than being played over the phone. He guessed it had been recorded in a corridor or long type of room because the background voices were distant and echoed. It was his view that if Lesley was being threatened or pressurised to make the tape, then there were people present who were whistling and in a happy frame of mind.

Len immediately telephoned Ronald to tell him this was the real thing, and Ronald in turn telephoned the incident room. For the next two hours the police set up a security ring around the area in Kidsgrove, while Ronald tried to kill time by finding out where Kidsgrove was on the map and how long it was likely to take him to get there. When he was finally asked to come over to the incident room, it took further time to fit him up with microphones so that he could, in an emergency, contact the police for help, not least if the kidnapper turned up at the telephone box for the ransom and then tried to kill or injure him.

At last, at 1.30 a.m. Ronald left the police station in his car for Kidsgrove with the money. Although the journey would usually take an hour and a quarter, by the time Ronald found Kidsgrove city centre and then the post office and the telephone kiosk, it was already 3 a.m. – much later than he would have liked. But he still wasn't out of the woods because once inside the kiosk there was no sign of the message. He felt along behind the backboard and then under the ledge – but nothing.

Perhaps there was another telephone box, but after a quick look around it was obvious this was the only one. Exhausted, his nerves stretched to breaking point, it even crossed his mind that this was another hoax. Last night it was a subway in Gloucester, tonight a telephone box in Kidsgrove. This time Ronald went back into the telephone box and rang the police on an emergency number he'd been given – the microphone system was only one-way so he couldn't talk to the police that way – and was invited to try again with the search and ring back in fifteen minutes.

He went on looking, with the same result, and with another telephone call was told to keep trying – and then, pushing his hand down the backboard as far as he could until he was nearly crying out with pain, Ronald's fingers brushed something poked so far behind the board that it wasn't surprising he'd missed it on the first two attempts.

Even then, it took another twenty minutes to extricate the message, again written on DYMO tape. He took the tape back to the car and wrote the message out in full on paper so that he could avoid the tortuous process of threading the tape through his fingers to check what he was meant to be doing. He then read the message out in full over the microphone to the police:

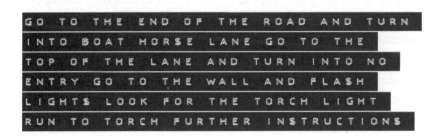

GO TO THE END OF THE ROAD AND TURN
INTO BOAT HORSE LANE GO TO THE
TOP OF THE LANE AND TURN INTO NO
ENTRY GO TO THE WALL AND FLASH
LIGHTS LOOK FOR THE TORCH LIGHT
RUN TO TORCH FURTHER INSTRUCTIONS

His hopes set high now that he'd found the message, despite being much later arriving in Kidsgrove than the kidnapper would have expected, Ronald drove down Boat Horse Lane and found the 'No Entry' sign into Bathpool Park. He drove into the car park as instructed, but saw no other vehicle, nor any wall. However, in the dark it was easy to miss the low wall where he was meant to stop and flash his lights.

Instead, he drove back out past the 'No Entry' signs and along the track passing under a bridge and beyond that a dam, the whole time looking for a wall at which he was meant to stop and flash his lights. He flashed his lights anyway and in the end, in a repeat performance of the previous night, got out of the car and started shouting to anyone who might hear him, just to give them the chance to come up and do the exchange. With no response here he drove on again to where there was a low wall on each side of the track and repeated the performance. He then went on further to another car park, and when there was still no response turned around and came back down the track continually flashing his lights.

By now it was 4 a.m. and he'd been in the park for at least half an hour.

As this went on with a running commentary from Ronald to the police through the microphone, radio contact with the police suddenly went dead. Their immediate fear was that Ronald had been attacked and the money taken off him. Three armed police officers were instructed to go into the park and see what was going on. To lose Ronald in the operation would be a catastrophe. The officers moved into the park and started up the track towards where they knew he was parked, but they'd only got 100 yards or so up the track when they saw a car's headlights coming down in the opposite direction, and to their relief they found it was Ronald. At the same time contact was renewed over the radio and the panic was over.

Earlier in the night, in the car park behind the 'No Entry' sign, where Ronald should have been under the instructions on the DYMO tape, a car occupied by a couple of young lovers was drawn up at the wall. Peter Shorto was a disc jockey who worked at a country club and whose nightly shift in the disco didn't finish until 2 a.m. His girlfriend Anne, later to become his wife, was working at the same club as a part-time receptionist and wages clerk.

Tonight she'd waited for him to finish his shift and then they'd had a drink and a snack together at the club. Bathpool Park was on the way home for Anne and the two of them often stopped there for a chat in the car before Peter dropped her off at home. They left the club at about 2.30 and reached the park a quarter of an hour later and parked as usual in the car park inside the entrance to the park, facing the low wall and the football pitch beyond it.

They'd only been sitting in the car a short time when they noticed a light flashing over the football pitch. The torch was being held level at them and was being switched on and off several times. It was aimed directly at them and was being waved in an arc. Peter had switched off all his lights on the car and it was a mystery why someone was flashing at them.

While all this was going on, a police patrol car drove into the park, around the pool and past the ski slope and then out of view. The car belonged to West Mercia Police who had no idea any operation was going on in the park and were on regular patrol.

About fifteen minutes after this a Ford Anglia van drove into the car park and stopped with its headlights on behind Peter's car and stayed there for about five minutes before driving on. After all these interruptions Peter and Anne stayed for about another fifteen minutes before driving on to Anne's home.

Looking at them through binoculars from the other side of the gulley, Donald Neilson wondered why no one was getting out of the car to come over to collect the instructions. Funnily enough the police car didn't faze him because he considered not even this lot would be crass enough to send in a patrol car lit up like a Christmas tree. He'd been out here often enough to know that local police made patrols from time to time and only stopped for a cigarette if there were no cars parked up, otherwise moved on rather than disturb the courting couples. In fact, there was part of him that had a bit of sympathy with the police on these night patrols, out in the small hours in the dark with not a lot going on when they could be tucked up in bed.

With the police car gone, Neilson kept flashing his torch, but with no result. Whittle must be sitting there in the car with the money and not budging. What did he expect, for him to go over and collect it? This now had all the signs of a trap. They knew where he was after all the light flashing. They were probably sitting in the back of the car just waiting for him to come over and then it would be all over. They would be armed and might even pick him off before he reached the car.

Neilson put down the torch. He'd had enough. This was the third time he'd tried to set up a rendezvous and each time it ended in nothing. If they couldn't make the effort then they could find her themselves. They'd got his car and now they knew where he was.

Time to move before they got him.

10

Donald Neilson was drifting into a purple haze. His fury at yet another delivery gone wrong was only tempered by his disbelief at a family with a 17-year-old daughter refusing to co-operate in the simplest way by picking up a telephone or delivering a bag of money. It wasn't difficult: when you wanted something enough you paid for it and you made sure the seller got the money. He had a 16-year-old daughter at home. He was a strict dad and didn't let her go out where she might run into temptation like drugs, or men with the wrong intention, but if anyone had dreamed up any operation like this involving his daughter then he'd get her back first and sort out the rest later – without the police.

What were they trying to prove? That by not doing anything they would smoke him out and catch him? Well, he'd shown them they were up against a professional, a trained soldier who would be welcomed into the higher ranks of the army, a man who wasn't afraid to kill when operations demanded it.

He'd been watching the parked car for some time. If it was Whittle then it was late, but then everything seemed to be late on this operation. He'd run late on the first evening, and he'd rung the house late tonight and got a male voice who was probably Whittle. Kidsgrove and the post office wasn't the easiest place in the world to find and that may have made him late. But he had a feeling about this car he was watching. It had driven into the car park as if it knew the place and drawn up in the same way at the wall – at home with everything was the way he'd put it. Then it sat there without flashing its lights. Why take all the trouble to turn up for the rendezvous and then not carry out the instructions? He'd watched the car through the binoculars and got the feeling – nothing much more than that, mind – that there were two people in the car. Anyway, he'd started flashing his torch at whoever it was without a response. Then, to cap it all, in comes a police car with sign on and does a circle and gets out as quickly as it comes in.

Then the car left, and just about when he thought that was it, another car drove past the entrance to the car park, hesitated for a moment and then drove on. Half an hour later another car appeared, driving much faster, and returned with the other car. Now that could have been his man, except it was all getting so late now he didn't know what to believe.

All the delay and the cars made him think more than ever that it was a trap being set up by the police. Perhaps even the first car was part of it. He should have gone up there and sorted them out. He was trained to ambush vehicles, although he had his doubts now about the .22 pistol that had failed to bring down that security guard at the depot yesterday. The shotgun was only any use close up – the hood and the shotgun put the fear in them. Not a piddly pistol – he had kept on running, the guard. The rifle would do the job, but that was at home and it was too heavy and too long for the bag.

He took the two cartridges out of the shotgun still across his knees, and put the safety catch back on the pistol before stowing them in the bag. He wouldn't be needing those any more. He'd made his mind up to shoot whoever it was who came up with the money. They knew too much about the pickup point now and would put two and two together

54

and have the area searched, including the drainage shafts. If it was Ronald Whittle he might not have told the police, and so getting rid of him would be the end of it for the time being.

The girl, of course, was a different matter. The truth was he still hadn't got the money and if he got rid of her then that really was it. He'd not be able to prove she was alive if it came to another attempt at a ransom. That was, if they hadn't found her by then. The odds were stacking up against him ever getting out of this.

He started taking things out of the bag – a Thermos with some chicken soup for the girl, a bag of barley sugar he was going to eat for energy with a couple of buns wrapped in polythene, a flask of tea that had gone cold days ago, a DYMO tape telling Whittle to drop the bag of money into the hole – and threw the lot out into the trees. What good had it all done him? – None at all. He'd lost his car, he had no money, he was wet, he was hungry, and he was dog-tired.

And he'd had to watch Whittle sit in his car with a policeman, laughing at him, waiting to jump him and find out where the girl was. Still, he hung on a few more minutes. It wasn't as if he was asking too much. He'd have to go home and tell his wife the big job, the big payday, was gone. Three years' work and preparation gone up in smoke, all because he picked a family who hadn't noticed their girl had gone, or who were so tight they couldn't bear to part with any money to get her back.

Perhaps they hadn't called the police. The security chap yesterday wasn't police. Perhaps they hadn't found his car after all – it might still be sitting there in the car park with all his gear – the tapes, the sleeping bag, the food. How could he have fed the girl with all the stuff in the car gone?

For all these reasons the operation had to come to an end. No one more than him would have liked to have brought it all off, but it wasn't to be. None of this was his fault; he'd remind anyone of this, if it came to it. He was blameless and a few questions would have to be asked as to why. Why hadn't they answered the phone, why hadn't they come over with the money, why hadn't they done damn all? He'd gone over it all a thousand times in his mind and now it was over.

He took a kick at a DYMO machine that had just fallen out of the bag and then pursued it, finally stamping on it until the plastic was in pieces and the tape crushed. Lot of bloody use all that was, they probably couldn't even read, illiterate bastards. How did Whittle make all that money running a business if he couldn't read? 'End of mission. Sorry to report it, sir, but enemy useless and abort is best option.'

'Very good, sergeant, carry on, and thanks for the report. You did your best and no one can ask for more. Don't forget, there's always next time. The most important thing is get out while you can.'

Donald Neilson stood up and saluted. He wasn't sure whom he was saluting, but it was towards the car park and over the railway. As if in reply, a passing train blew its whistle and rattled through into the tunnel. It must be moving towards dawn now and time he got things wrapped up. The police might already be moving in and he couldn't hang around.

He ran over to the glory hole and pulled back the metal cover. After climbing through the hole and positioning himself on the ladder, he switched on his torch and pulled the cover back over his head without taking his usual trouble in pulling the cover right over to avoid detection. It was nearly dawn, nobody would be around, and he wasn't going to be very long anyway.

He sloshed through the water on the first level, making sure he kept the bag dry, and then down to the second level and the dry landing where he kept the tape recorder and the primus stove. Then the last leg down to the lower platform where the girl – the girl who was going to earn him £50,000 – lay as usual in her sleeping bag.

But was that her? As he looked down all he could see was a mummified figure the same shape as the girl with her long hair but distorted by whatever was lying over her. His immediate fear was that it could be a policeman in drag in some set-up to catch him right at this last hour.

Lesley had heard him coming down and put on the lantern at the bottom of the ladder. She put the polythene sheet that wrapped the emergency blanket bag over her to protect her from the pieces of rust and debris that always fell on her when he came down the ladder. She could see him hesitating as she removed the sheet, and the look in his eyes that told her it had all gone wrong. They were bloodshot and not focusing. She moved over a few inches to her right to allow him to stand

56

at the foot of the ladder, his boots dripping wet and his face smeared with mud or camouflage. He wore a flat cap, and his filthy coat and stubble made him look nothing more than a tramp who'd lost his way in the tunnels.

Neilson stood there on the platform, breathing hard with the exertion of sudden movement after the hours of sitting among the trees waiting. 'Operation over,' he said at last.

Lesley looked up at him. 'That's good,' she said and tried to smile.

'Not good,' he grunted. 'No money.'

'Why not?' she asked.

'No money,' he repeated.

'I'm sure they want to give the money to you,' she said.

But he wasn't listening and started reaching over her to pick up odd items from the platform, like the brandy bottle and the slippers, and started throwing them over the side where they fell with a splash into the water below. These were followed by the polythene sheet and blanket. 'Where's the soup?' he barked.

'I've got it here in the flask in the sleeping bag. I'm keeping it warm,' said Lesley.

'Give it me,' he demanded, and bent down with his back to her to see what other odds and ends he could jettison over the side.

Lesley leant forward slightly to reach down inside the sleeping bag for the Thermos flask. As she pulled it back up she started to lose her balance and felt herself going over the side. She thrust out an arm but the inside of the bag was silky smooth and it took a split second to soundlessly slide over the edge. The wire around her neck snagged on a stanchion on the platform, pulled up taut and brought her up short of the floor of the shaft by a few inches.

Neilson turned to find her gone. He crawled to the edge of the platform, squatted with one foot on the platform and the other on a stone ledge on the other side of the tunnel, and shone his torch down into Lesley's face as she swung there, one of her arms moving. Her eyes looked up at him for a couple of seconds as the noose bit into her neck, dilated and then closed.

He knew she was dead and didn't even try to haul her back up.

Her final indignity was her sleeping bag, weighted with the Thermos flask still inside, sliding down to expose her naked body, over her feet and down into the stream below where it was carried away in the current.

Neilson turned around, decided to leave the other sleeping bag and blanket where they were on the platform, and ran up the ladder for the last time as fast as his short legs could carry him.

This was not part of the plan.

11

Donald Neilson wasn't in a rush to get home. All he wanted to do was get out of Bathpool Park. The money could wait. Everything could wait as far as he was concerned. He picked up his bag and started to walk down from the glory hole. A car was coming into Bathpool Park – he could see its lights. He ran down the mound towards the disused railway. He fell badly and dropped the bag, and the contents, another Thermos of soup and some buns, spilt out on to the ground.

For a few minutes he lay there motionless, his heart beating against the grass. Now he could see the headlights of the car coming along the bottom of the ski slope towards him in the park. They must have found out what was going on and surrounded him. They'd arrest him and then find the girl. He scooped some of the contents of the bag off the ground and started running.

Then, what was that? Barking, it was dogs, they'd run him to earth like a fox. He ran faster, in the opposite direction this time. This is what he trained for all these years. He could outrun them and he knew it. He didn't even bother to go back and fetch the holdall from the bushes with the soup and sweets and few other odds and ends that he was going to take down to the girl if he'd got the money. He even left his precious pair of binoculars near the glory hole where Whittle was going to drop the case with the money.

He was going to walk away from it all. By leaving everything there he'd show his contempt for them. Three years' planning for nothing, all because of them. They could have it all, the car and everything in it, the soup and the sweets that would have kept her alive. No one was going to say he hadn't thought of her every comfort, down to the Elastoplast around the noose.

If he ever did this again, and he doubted now he ever would, he'd pick a family with more money and not so obsessed with catching him, who valued their daughter more than money and didn't run off to the police, although he still wasn't quite sure they had told the police even now. There was nothing to connect him with the post office jobs, no fingerprints and no one had seen his face, except the girl. What could she have done except give them one of those stupid identikit pictures that weren't any help to anyone.

Could he have finished her off if she hadn't slipped off the platform? She reminded him too much of Kathryn – it'd be like shooting your own daughter. They'd find her soon enough now. He'd liked her. They'd got on. She didn't try to cause trouble like the other lot in the post offices. You had to respect that.

They'd have got the car and gone through the tapes and gone to the zoo and probably found the rope he was going to use to pull the money over the wall. But what had happened? He'd outsmarted them by changing the venue the very next day to Kidsgrove.

He walked to the railway station, joining other workers for the early morning train. The police wouldn't be looking for him here, they'd be out on the roads setting up road blocks and all that nonsense. He looked the part now walking for the train, unshaven, cloth-capped, bit scruffy.

Approaching Bradford he couldn't help thinking how it should have been. There should have been a bag stuffed full of the money that was going to give him a holiday, buy his wife some decent clothes, stuff for the house, a new car or van for work. Instead, what was it? Bloody failure as usual; that look from Irene as he walked through the door that said, 'perhaps this time', and the look from him that told it all.

He was afraid of his daughter Kathryn guessing what was going on, but then she was more likely to guess if he suddenly came into money. Funny that he was still strict about her going out in the evening in case she met the wrong type of people, though God knows he was about the last type he'd want his daughter to meet. He'd now left a girl his daughter's age dead at the bottom of a drain – that could have been Kathryn, couldn't it? Her mother could have been Irene, still wondering where she was and whether she was alive.

He'd never told his family that he'd failed basic training when he joined the army, the only one in the intake to fail and the only one to be back-squadded. There was a photo of their wedding in the front room at home of him in his uniform with Irene looking lovely – the bride and her military man, the idiot who couldn't even pass basic training.

All the same, things might have been different if he'd stayed in the army. Irene wanted him out because she wasn't seeing much of him, but how much was she seeing of him now? Sometimes he'd be out for nights at a time; he could explain it by saying they were jobs around the country, which in a way they were. He'd given her a whole stack of postal orders with instructions to get rid of them if anything happened to him. Burn them, he'd said.

He'd killed three people in the post-office raids: two postmasters and one husband of a postmistress. He wasn't sure about the man at Freightliner, he seemed to have got through it. Unforeseen circumstance, that was it, and any court would understand that they were accidents. A warning shot for the first and he got in the way. But the rest of them, that was different because each one of them hadn't done what they were told. Self-defence. They'd tried it on and found out you didn't mess with anyone like him who was military trained. They'd seen the gun. They knew what would happen. He had photos at home of him and the wife and daughter out on exercises in the woods, him in the jeep and Irene playing dead half out of the jeep and Kathryn throwing a stick bomb. It all worked beautiful then and it would have worked beautiful if those idiots on the raids hadn't tried it on.

61

The Whittles had tried it on by not answering the phone and being late and then sitting in the car expecting him to come over for a chat instead of handing over the money. Now they realised what they were up against. No second chances and no excuses.

Dawn was up now. He hadn't slept for forty-eight hours but he was trained to do that. He'd get home and get some kip and be ready again for duty. Irene would wash his kit and he'd explain they hadn't come up with the money. They'd let him down. But that was life, you win some you lose some.

He was drifting off in the train and glad he wasn't driving. Do that on the road and you'd likely kill someone …

12

On 23 January 1976, eight days after the Freightliner shooting, a member of the public walked into Dudley police station and rang the bell on the desk. It was Friday evening and he was smartly dressed in a suit, hat and coat. He brought the chill of the winter's evening in with him.

The duty sergeant appeared with a mug of tea in his hand. 'Yes sir. How can I help?'

'The thing is, Sergeant, this might not be anything, but I've noticed a car in the car park I use opposite the bus station.'

'I see, sir, and there's something unusual about the car?' asked the sergeant, taking a sip at his tea. It was Friday evening and you always got a few of these end of week callers, usually had a couple in the pub after work.

'The car hasn't actually been moved for the whole week. I know that because I use the car park every day and I park next to the car. It's got a bit dirty over the week, and it just shows how much muck a car collects in only a week.'

The sergeant opened the logbook and started writing down the details. 'Could I have the make of the car, sir?'

'I can do better than that, Sergeant, I can give you the registration number,' said the man, bringing out a piece of paper. 'The number is TTV 454H. It's a Morris 1100.'

'Thank you, sir,' said the sergeant. 'Do you recall the colour of the car?'

'Darkish green, I think, although it's hard to tell because it's so dirty. The thing is, Sergeant, I believe it's been *abandoned.*' The man might have been describing a child lost in the snow.

'I see, sir. Anything else about the car?'

'There is, as a matter of fact. I made a little window in the window, if you see what I mean, through the condensation, and I could see one or two pretty strange things. By the way, those will be my fingerprints on the window. No, there was a coil of rope, what looks like a foam mattress, a pair of trousers and, most suspicious of all, a pair of lady's knickers on the front passenger seat. What do you make of all that, Sergeant?'

The sergeant finished what he was writing in the log. 'I don't know, sir, but we'll have a look. If the car's gone by Monday you can be sure it's been taken care of.'

A check showed the registration was false, and when the police reached the car it was obvious the tax disc belonged to another vehicle and had been altered in amateur fashion. Inside the car, beside the rope and a pair of knickers that had been used as a cleaning cloth, was a tape recorder and cassette, a tin of petrol, a bottle of Lucozade, a bag of barley sugar sweets, and four brown envelopes.

Inside the numbered envelopes was a series of instructions on DYMO tape to go to a number of telephone boxes in the Dudley area, ending up at the Freightliner depot where there were instructions to find more directions taped to a lamp post.

The big embarrassment for the police was that the abandoned car belonging to Lesley Whittle's kidnapper was only 250 yards from the scene of the Freightliner shooting and had been found by a member of the public instead of the police in their search. Even then, it took the police days to find the instructions taped to the lamp post, and this was the result of an intensive search in daylight. Had this been night-time, as originally intended, the chances were Ronald Whittle would never have found the instructions. Meanwhile, the messages intended for Ronald were found one by one in the various telephone boxes, confirming that the tapes found in the car were simply duplicates.

The message found on the lamp post directed that Ronald should 'CROSS ROAD AND CAR PARK GO RIGHT TO GATE NUMBER 8', and while this was obviously referring to the gates into Dudley Zoo, the reality was it was impossible to identify Gate Number 8. The gates weren't numbered, and even the zoo staff could refer to four gates only. Ronald Whittle would have had no hope of ever finding the gate had he ever had the opportunity.

The mystery of Gate 8 was solved days later when police found a DYMO tape in a stretch of wasteland a distance away from the Freightliner's lamp post reading, 'INSTRUCTIONS AT END OF ROPE.' The question of what rope was only solved when it turned out that a day or two after the shooting, police had been alerted to another suspicious car in the zoo car park, and though the car had gone by the time the police got there they did find a 250ft length of rope. They never found any more instructions, but the police could assume now that the rope was going to be used to haul the case of money over the wall, and allow the kidnapper to disappear in the night into the honeycomb of caves and tunnels that made up the zoo grounds.

Alternatively, the kidnapper would have had the easy option of shooting the person with the money in this comparative wilderness and making off with the bag.

Meanwhile, it hadn't taken the police long to examine the six spent .22 cartridges left behind by the gunman when he shot Gerald Smith in the car park, together with three live rounds, and found that this was the same gun that had killed two sub-postmasters in Accrington, Lancashire and Langley, Berkshire.

For the first time they knew they were dealing with the Black Panther.

Later on in the evening, after the Morris 1100 was found and the cassette tape tested for fingerprints, Booth and his team slotted the cassette into a tape recorder and pushed the play button. It was a girl's voice talking in what sounded like an empty room. She repeated a set of instructions three times in a clear voice, 'Go to the M6 north to Junction 10 and then on to the A454 towards Walsall. Instructions are taped under the shelf in the telephone box.' The voice was clearly Lesley Whittle's, and she added on the tape a message to her mother that there was no need to worry, that she was okay, and that she'd got a bit wet but was quite dry now. She finished by saying she was being treated very well.

This is the tape that would have been played to Ronald on that first night in Dudley in the shopping centre, had he been there to answer the phone at midnight, or on the second evening had Neilson not had to abandon his call after shooting Gerald Smith.

13

Establishing the link with the Black Panther gave the police an insight as to the type of character they were looking for: a man who graduated from burglary to armed robbery, from armed robbery to murder, and now to kidnapping a teenage girl. His crimes were becoming more violent and more adventurous.

In the last few years there had been a series of raids around the country on sub-post offices that were beginning to carry certain hallmarks in the way they were carried out. Usually the intruder gained access to the property in the early hours of the morning by drilling two neat holes in the metal window frames and releasing the window latch with a wire. Once he was in he would set up an escape route by opening a door and then look for the post office room inside the house. There would then follow a cursory search for the keys to the office door and the safe, and sometimes this was successful and the postmaster and his family asleep upstairs would not have to be disturbed. They were the lucky ones.

If the keys couldn't be found then the Panther, dressed in black from head to foot with a hood with slits for his eyes, would start his progress upstairs. Once or twice he was able to get into the bedroom where husband and wife lay asleep and go through a pair of trousers or jacket, or feel his way across a dressing table or chest of drawers, until he found the keys. Then it was downstairs, open the safe and fill a holdall with the cash and stamps, and off without disturbing anyone.

But inevitably this was all too good to last.

In the early hours of Friday, 15 February 1974, at a sub-post office in a suburb of Harrogate, 18-year-old Richard Skepper was asleep in bed. He was awoken by a double-barrelled shotgun being poked in his face by someone wearing a black hood and talking in an odd squeaky voice, demanding the safe keys. Richard knew his father usually kept them in the cupboard under the stairs and told the intruder, who then tied up his hands and feet and put a thick plaster around his mouth as a gag.

But the intruder couldn't find the keys and ten minutes later was back in Richard's bedroom, untied him and ordered him to come downstairs and find the keys. Richard realised they weren't there and, with gag removed, explained they were probably upstairs in a drawer in his parents' bedroom. He was then ordered to go and get them and so, chaperoned by the man in black, Richard crept into his parents' bedroom while the intruder waited in the doorway.

This awoke both parents and Donald Skepper turned on a light to reveal the bedroom suddenly filled with people, his son Richard blinking in the light and a man dressed in black with a hood standing in the doorway with a sawn-off shotgun. The gunman, instead of making a run for it, told Donald to turn out the light, but when he refused to do so attempted to turn off the switch at the door, only to find this was the main bedroom light, illuminating the room.

Donald Skepper, keeping his composure, asked what the intruder wanted and was told by Richard it was the safe keys. Had Neilson been handed the keys at this point, he would have taken ten minutes tying each of the Skepper family up, probably using Richard as the most co-operative to do this, and then finally gagged each of them before going downstairs to empty the safe.

Instead Donald Skepper sprang from his bed and shouted to Richard, 'Let's get him!' This time Neilson wasn't willing to argue or put up a fight, a fight he probably would have lost against two men, and he pulled the trigger. The shot hit Donald in the heart, and he staggered back, dying, into his wife's arms.

Neilson ran back downstairs and, still without the keys to open the safe, grabbed his bag and fled. No one had seen his face and he'd parked the car some distance from the house, and so the chances of being recognised or pursued were minimal.

A month later there was another burglary, in Staffordshire, with the tell-tale hallmarks of the two holes drilled in the window. But, by a fluke, the postmaster had left the safe keys downstairs and the intruder helped himself to the contents of the safe without having to trouble the family asleep upstairs. The postmaster may have lost over £4,000 in the raid but probably saved his and his family's lives by being less conscientious than some of his colleagues.

Then, in the early hours of 6 September 1974, another Friday, it was the turn of the sub-post office in the village of Higher Baxendale in Accrington, with two bored holes in a window frame and the telephone wires cut. No keys were conveniently left downstairs this time and so the intruder made his way upstairs into the bedroom of postmaster Derek Anstin and his wife Marion. Both were awoken by the sight and sound of the intruder and Derek Anstin, an ex-Royal Marine, threw back the bedclothes and boldly launched himself at the hooded figure. There was an ear-splitting crash as Anstin was shot at point-blank range. Anstin, badly wounded, in a final effort threw the man downstairs, but then received a single bullet from a .22 pistol fired from the foot of the stairs. The intruder escaped through the same window and Derek Anstin was dead by the time he reached hospital.

On Monday, 11 November 1974, postmistress Peggy Grayland and her husband Sidney were following their usual evening routine in preparing to go home from their sub-office at Langley, between Birmingham and Wolverhampton. Peggy heard a bump come from the storeroom at the back of the house when her husband was meant to be collecting the car. She went into the storeroom to find her husband on his back on the floor, warning her, 'Watch out, Peggy. I've been hit.' The next thing she saw was a man framed in the doorway, not wearing a hood, coming towards her, and that was the last she remembered. Sidney died of his wound, a shot fired by a .22 calibre gun, while Peggy barely escaped with her life after being repeatedly hit around the head with a pistol butt.

The police found the safe door open with the keys in the lock. Only £861 had been taken in cash, while £19,000 worth of postal orders, premium bonds, savings stamps and postage stamps had been left behind. Also the robber had failed to notice a wad of £600 cash lying in Peggy Grayland's handbag next to the safe.

Despite the only shot being the one to Sidney's heart, the police found five spent .22 cartridges on the floor of the storeroom and a number of live rounds. The only explanation they could give was that the gunman was wildly trigger happy in the dark, attacking Sidney and firing four rounds that missed their target.

One thing was clear now. Whoever was carrying out these raids killed his victims as the norm, but in doing so was taking quite disproportionate risks in shooting his victims for a few thousand pounds here or there, and sometimes nothing at all. Sooner or later he would be caught and spend the rest of his life in prison.

The decision for Donald Neilson, driving long distances between these sub-post offices and home and giving himself lots of time to think, was whether to carry on in this vein or whether to go for a more ambitious target, where he could combine the brains he felt he had, his military training and his meticulous planning, and go for the big one, the venture into the unknown with one big pay-off, with less risk of being seen off by these lunatics risking their lives for a few paltry thousand pounds.

An alternative like kidnapping, for instance ...

14

While Donald Neilson could not be credited as an original thinker, he was to a fault a methodical planner who naturally thought in duplicate and didn't like the idea of risk. This might sound paradoxical for a man who went out with a sawn-off shotgun and a .22 pistol in his bag, but if you wore a hood and gloves when carrying out a crime then identification was difficult, fingerprints non-existent, and the risk of a victim getting the better of you if he fought back was removed if you shot him.

What Neilson didn't like was sloppy thinking, people who hadn't planned things properly and who hadn't done their homework. If the army taught him one thing, it was that you had to plan – to rehearse each move and see how long it took, how far one crime scene was from another, whether you moved at night or by day, how your victims led their lives and their routines – so that by the time you came to execute the operation you knew all about them.

This is why Neilson was dismayed by the kidnapping of Muriel McKay in December 1969 as a precedent in the way it was carried out. He was, however, intrigued by the idea of a single payout in the form of a ransom rather than fiddling around with the odd few thousand pounds here and there after months of planning a post office robbery. Why not spend a couple of years planning an operation that would pay ten times as much and allow you to buy a decent house, have a couple of holidays and pay off the bills, with enough left over to prevent having to do it all again – paid for by people who wouldn't miss the money anyway?

Above all, it gave you class. It was the difference between being an officer and a squaddie.

This was the main motive for Arthur Hosein in kidnapping Muriel McKay – he wanted to be seen as the squire of the village, a member of the local gentry, the man who would command respect – not bad for a first generation immigrant from Trinidad.

But Neilson didn't like the way the kidnapping was carried out. First of all, the Hosein brothers abducted the wrong woman on 29 December 1969, thinking they had got the newspaper baron Rupert Murdoch's wife when instead they had captured his vice chairman's wife. Secondly, they asked for too much money – £1 million – a sum that couldn't be raised in cash at short notice. No need to be so greedy – ask for a sensible amount that could be stuffed into one bag. Amateurish and rushed, too little time taken in the planning.

While the Hoseins had managed to get the right car, a Rolls-Royce belonging to the Murdochs, they hadn't realised it had been loaned to Mrs McKay while the Murdochs were on holiday in Australia. The Hoseins followed the car back to a house in Wimbledon, which they assumed was the Murdochs' house.

At first the police couldn't quite believe this was a kidnap; they thought Mrs McKay might have left her husband, or that this was a stunt put up to advertise the Murdoch takeover of the *News of the World*. Some of the items strewn around the house looked like theatre props, the contents of Mrs McKay's handbag tipped on to the stairs, a length of bandage, a coil of string and a meat cleaver.

Any hope the police had of keeping the affair and negotiations discreet were blown when the *Sun* newspaper, at Mr McKay's request, made the story front-page news. The McKays' phone line became jammed with calls from the press, well-wishers and various cranks hoping to make a quick fortune.

The ransom demand was reduced to £500,000 after a few days, with instructions to drop it off in two bags on a garage forecourt. The bags were spotted by local residents, who reported them to local police, who in turn collected the bags and took them to the police station. While this was happening a Volvo carrying the Hosein brothers stopped on the forecourt to see what was going on, keeping its distance from the bags, only to be told by an attendant that they couldn't park there and to move on. The only positive outcome was the police noticing the Volvo car cruising repeatedly past, as it had on another abortive drop, and the car was then traced to the Hoseins' pig farm on the Hertfordshire–Essex border. There they found the notepad used to send the ransom demands, and Arthur Hosein's fingerprints on the demands themselves. The only thing missing was a body, and in the end the assumption was that Mrs McKay had been fed to the pigs.

While this operation was not the most impressive precedent Donald Neilson had for his attempt, it was about the only available one in the UK as the crime not been attempted here in recent times. He could see the anonymity of phone boxes had their uses in making calls, but the idea of a drop at a phone was far too dangerous if the police were involved – best to arrange somewhere where it would be remote enough to spot the police if they were tailing the operation, or somewhere he could make a quick and easy getaway once he'd picked up the money.

The other lesson was don't use paper ransom demands with your fingerprints all over them. Neilson had already learnt to wear gloves in anything to do with his crimes, whether it was in the preparation or the execution. Some form of printing would be needed for any messages, and that excluded typewriters that were just about as traceable as fingerprints. Third lesson was, don't use a car in all this with number plates that can be traced straightaway by the police. A stolen car might do, perhaps even manufacturing your own plates.

There was a further lesson here. Best not to return the victim – she would recognise you again, unless you were going to wear a hood all the time and speak in a disguised voice. What was the point of returning her

– you'd got the money and releasing her would certainly end in you being caught. Neilson had learnt his lesson the hard way – dead men don't talk, and if you got rid of the body then that was it.

The Hoseins had only succeeded on one of those counts and that wasn't enough. They hadn't been trained, they weren't fit, and they were amateurs in a professional's world.

Donald Neilson wasn't an amateur – every successful raid made him more confident, and he had all the time in the world to plan this one. The Hoseins had got their target from a television programme telling the world how rich Rupert Murdoch was. Neilson would keep an eye on the television and newspapers to see who was around now with money to spare, especially if he could find someone who deserved losing it. He didn't mind taking post office money because that didn't hurt anyone. The only people who got hurt there were the ones who tried to stop him.

When it came to military careers, Arthur Hosein's time in national service had been about as bad as Donald Neilson's. Hosein was court-martialled for desertion and described by one of his officers as the worst soldier it had been his misfortune to command. Neilson failed his basic training and had to take it again, although national service did give him a purpose in life and an enthusiasm for firearms.

The Hoseins using phone boxes to remain anonymous worked while making calls, but led to the same complications in starting a trail around the countryside, with police in various disguises swamping the drop zones and putting off the kidnappers. In the case of the Hoseins they made the drop too exposed, with members of the public randomly picking up the money and causing the kidnappers to move on, while Neilson made his trail so complicated no one could follow it, in daylight let alone in the dark.

What Arthur Hosein and Donald Neilson did have in common were fatal character flaws: each of them were small men with big ideas. Had Arthur opened his farm as a bed and breakfast, things might have gone better. If Neilson had stuck to burglary and robbing post offices, then he might have gone on getting away with it. But their ambitions overtook them.

One should also feel some sympathy for the police trying to solve crimes in which they had little or no experience, in a blaze of publicity where every move is plastered across the front page of national newspapers, aware that the first demand made from the kidnappers is that the police are not to be involved, when it is blindingly obvious to everyone that you *are* involved, and as such losing the chance of building up any trust with the kidnappers that might have led to a successful outcome.

Had the money ever reached the Hoseins they would have discovered all but the top layers of the cash were counterfeit and that they'd been dumped with Monopoly money in bags that were bugged. At least the money in Neilson's case was real, in a bag that wasn't bugged.

All this went some way to explain why kidnap was not a popular crime in this country.

Kidnappers in America at this time weren't faring much better, and one case in December 1968 might well have come to Neilson's attention, for example in an article in the May issue of *Reader's Digest* in 1972 as he waited in the doctor's surgery. It had a few similarities with the Whittle case. Barbara Mackle was a 20-year-old student who was kidnapped in the presence of her mother in a motel room in Decatur, Georgia. Gary Krist and his accomplice took Barbara by car to a pine wood where they buried her alive in a fibreglass coffin. An air pump was fitted to the coffin, together with a couple of air pipes to let her breathe, water with added sedatives and a supply of food. For light she was given a battery-operated torch.

Krist then demanded a ransom of $500,000 from Barbara's wealthy father. The first drop, anticipating the Neilson aborted drop, was abandoned by the kidnappers when two policemen, unaware of the operation in progress, drove past. But the police found their abandoned car, complete with documents identifying the kidnappers and a photograph of Barbara in her coffin with a placard reading 'Kidnapped' lying across her. The second drop was successful, and Krist gave enough directions to allow a police task force of 100 officers, some digging with their bare hands, to find the coffin and Barbara alive but dehydrated. Krist and his accomplice were subsequently caught and sentenced.

Both Krist's and Neilson's victims, one 17 and the other barely out of her teens, had to endure the terrible ordeal of spending their captivity underground, in one case literally buried alive, in the dark and not knowing if they would survive.

15

After listening to the tape on 23 January of Lesley Whittle giving her last instructions as to where to take the money, Bob Booth felt sure she was trying to give a hint in her last words when she said she got a bit wet but now she was dry, and that hint was something to do with Bathpool Park. Otherwise, why bring Ronald Whittle so far from Dudley and Kidderminster as the previous scenes of activity?

So far, he hadn't ordered a thorough search of the park because doing so would have told the kidnapper that the police knew about the abortive drop at the park and were colluding with Ronald. After all, the kidnapper had made it quite clear in his message that any involvement of the police or other tricks would result in Lesley's death, and if this was the Black Panther then they knew he meant it.

Booth therefore needed some excuse to search the park that didn't necessarily suggest a direct link to Ronald as his source of information. The BBC coming up to do an interview with Ronald about the case gave Booth his chance, and an ingenious plot was hatched whereby Ronald would let it slip in the interview with Tom Mangold that he'd tried to hand over the money at Bathpool Park but that the handover had been unsuccessful. Once it came to Booth's turn to be interviewed by the BBC and asked about the unsuccessful rendezvous, Booth exploded with thespian fury at apparently not knowing about this and stormed out of the interview. The interview was on Sunday, 2 March 1975 and by the Tuesday the search was organised, followed by early success when a local headmaster reported that a couple of 11-year-old pupils had found a piece of DYMO tape saying 'DROP SUITCASE INTO HOLE', in undergrowth two days after the kidnapping. Then a lantern-type torch was found by other children inside a gap in the bars of the entrance to one of the shafts known locally as the 'glory hole'. The children remembered the piece of DYMO tape stuck to the lantern and this presumably was the message to drop the case into the hole.

Some girls out riding found a pair of binoculars in the area, together with a green tartan holdall, a hammer and a coat. Some other boys found two Thermos flasks, one half-full of chicken soup, and two sugar buns wrapped in polythene bags. The pieces of the jigsaw were starting to fit together.

All this meant that having searched the area overground, they needed now to move underground. So on the afternoon of Thursday, 6 March the underground search began. DC Maskery, a local scene-of-crimes officer, and Sergeant Perriton put a ladder through the gap in the railings to the glory hole and climbed down 40ft to a whole new subterranean world. A 5ft diameter tunnel carried away water, and directly under the entrance to the glory hole was an assortment of rubbish including a DYMO tape machine and a roll of Elastoplast tape.

Next day, they followed the line of this tunnel to the next inspection hatch, although this didn't reveal anything, but it was at the next cover nearest the entrance to the park where things started to get interesting. This was on a small hillock to the right of the track leading from the car park to the ski slope. The cover was secured by a bolt that seemed to be in the right position but was in fact only finger tight.

A local authority worker with breathing apparatus went down the ladder first, to check the air was safe to breathe because this shaft was part of an old coal mine complex. The first level appeared to be safe and DC Maskery and Sergeant Perriton made their way down the ladder to a depth of about 22ft, and then down another ladder a further 23ft. It was at this level, a short distance from the landing, that they found a cassette recorder, a large envelope and a packet of smaller brown envelopes, two writing pads, a paintbrush and a pot of white paint. They also found in the cache a roll of Elastoplast and a number of batteries.

Maskery climbed down a further ladder for about 9ft and at the bottom of this third level was a narrow metal platform 2ft wide, stretching in length across the full diameter of the shaft. Here he found a strip of yellow foam on the platform, and a maroon sleeping bag rolled up in a polythene bag to form what looked like a pillow. Hanging up to one side of the ladder was a blue dressing gown.

Secured to the bottom of the ladder was a metal ligature, which was looped around the ladder and secured by three clamps, each one with three securing nuts. The ligature wire then led from the bottom of the ladder across the sleeping bag to the edge of the platform, where it had snagged on a stanchion supporting the platform, and then disappeared over the side.

Maskery, holding the torch and doing his best not to fall over the side of the platform, looked over the edge. He was looking directly down on the top of a human head. The neck was secured to the other end of the wire by another ligature held by three clamps, and below that hung the naked body of a young girl.

Everything was very still, and the only noise was rushing water where a stream ran across the base of the shaft. The feet of the suspended body were only inches from the bottom of the shaft.

Maskery, in all of his career as a police officer, had never faced anything like this. He felt like an intruder, as if he'd walked into someone's grave. Then he felt terribly sad, sad for the girl, and sorry that anyone could do such a sad thing to another human being. He turned and, shining his torch up the ladder, made his own slow ascent to the surface to tell the world the search was over.

16

The news that Lesley's body had been found was received by Bob Booth and his team with mixed feelings. On one hand elation that they had her and could now start concentrating on finding the kidnapper, and on the other a feeling of what might have been if they'd been able to search Bathpool Park in depth earlier without running the risk that the kidnapper would know they were involved.

From a professional point of view, it meant that Booth had lost the murder case because the body was located in Staffordshire. At a press conference announcing the finding of Lesley's body, Booth rather rashly announced that they would find the kidnapper within twenty-four hours. This assumption was based on the conclusion, falsely as it turned out, that the perpetrator would be a past or present worker in the drainage system with inside knowledge of the layout of the various drains and tunnels. It turned out there were a lot more workers than was first thought. The positive side of the announcement carried the chance of smoking out the kidnapper if he took fright and suddenly left home.

But Neilson stayed put, probably safe in the knowledge that even if his family knew they would never tell the police.

The pathologist's report stated that Lesley's body was dehydrated, and there were no signs of her having consumed food in at least the last three days before her death. Additionally, there were no marks on her back or shoulders to suggest that there had been any effort to pull her back up on to the rusty platform after she fell, and so the implication was she was either alone when she went over the side in a desperate effort to find food or water, or that she'd been pushed over and left to die. Further searches found her sleeping bag had dropped into the stream under the platform and been washed away through the drain into the canal, and this implied that when she fell she was in her sleeping bag which then slipped off her body into the stream below.

The police also found strips of Elastoplast 3in wide, some with eyebrow hairs attached, that had been used as a blindfold, and her slippers that had been washed out into the canal. Also a brandy bottle, a pair of trousers, socks and Thermos flasks, one of which was still inside the sleeping bag, although whether the bottle and clothing were intended for the victim or the kidnapper as he prepared the hiding place in the days leading up to the abduction was unclear. Also in the shaft were various pieces of tape-recording equipment and DYMO tape, together with an airmail pad bearing the impression of the instructions to Lesley for her telephone message telling them to go to the Kidsgrove telephone box.

The airmail pad was in the dry culvert on the second floor, along with a notepad that gave the police their only fingerprint of the Panther inside the front cover. Despite all his meticulous preparation over the years, this was the one and only time he left a fingerprint, another morale booster for the police – they may not yet have got their man, but when they did they'd know for certain that they'd got the right one.

Meanwhile, on a Sunday in the previous February, 11-year-old Paul Inskip, his 12-year-old brother, Simon, and two of their friends had been playing in Bathpool Park instead of playing football because it was raining. They'd run into the woods in the park, climbing trees and picking conkers. On the way back they played around what they called 'the sewers', and particularly around the glory hole, which was always an attraction because you could look down through the bars at the murky water inside the shaft. Only, on this occasion, one of the bars was broken and inside was a purple and black square torch. Some tape was stuck to the side of the torch, with a word on the tape like 'DOCTOR'.

As he found the torch, Simon had also found an orange tape gun in the grass and he and his friends each had a go with it. When they'd done this he threw it down the glory hole into the water. Paul reached in and pulled out the torch from behind the bars. There was some other writing on the tape but Simon pulled it off from the torch and threw it away down the bank. They played with the torch, switching it on and off in their games, and when the games were over Paul took the torch back home with him. It was only in March when the police officially searched the park and appealed to anyone who might have found anything in the area that Paul went to the police station and showed them exactly where he'd found the torch at the top of the glory hole.

And it wasn't just the Inskip brothers who were picking up the debris left by Neilson. Other children out riding or playing in the area found a pair of binoculars, a hammer, a stopwatch and a holdall near the main shaft entrance, together with a couple of vacuum flasks and sugar buns in a plastic bag. All were found just before or just after the night Ronald made his abortive attempt to leave the ransom money in the park.

Another interesting fact came to light in the police investigation. Back on 24 September 1974, four months before the kidnapping, the police on routine patrol had found an Escort van parked inside a farm driveway in the Bathpool Park area. The van contained the by now familiar list of yellow foam rubber mattress, kettle and saucepan, torch, tinned food and tartan holdall. The van was apparently being lived in and was stolen.

The police decided to let down the rear tyres and keep an eye on it. When they returned to the vehicle from time to time they noticed the contents starting to disappear, and later railway workers found some of the equipment being stored near the railway line with a dark, short man hanging around the area with a 1100 car. The van was impounded but, in light of later events, had clearly been used by Neilson as a base to explore Bathpool Park. It would have been used in the kidnap itself had it not been discovered by the police, who unwittingly delayed the kidnap by a few months while Neilson found another vehicle and replaced the equipment he'd lost.

A search was organised using potholers and cavers at Dudley Zoo when it was found that one of the caves behind what the kidnapper had called 'Gate 8' went right into the rocks and emerged in Forest Road, allowing a man just enough room to crawl through as an escape route. This was confirmed by locals having seen the stolen green 1100 in a road near this exit in Forest Road. So, had Ronald Whittle got as far as the zoo and ever identified 'Gate 8', found the rope and attached the bag of money, then once Neilson had hauled the bag over the wall he could have made his escape through the cave to Forest Road and his waiting car. This could have happened without much trouble, even if the police had been waiting with Ronald, because by the time they'd got over or through the wall, their quarry would be long gone. Even in the event of them getting to the other side of the wall fairly quickly and giving chase, Neilson would only have had to blast a pursuer with his shotgun and kill or injure him, blocking the narrow space that allowed crawling only, to emerge in Forest Road like a rabbit from his burrow.

17

The police now had a body, boxes full of forensic evidence and sightings of the suspect, but no suspect himself. The kidnap had taken place in Highley, one attempted ransom drop in Dudley and another in Kidsgrove, and it was Kidsgrove where Lesley's body was eventually found. The investigations now involved two police authorities, West Mercia and Staffordshire, and the rivalry between the two forces wasn't helping matters.

Finding the Black Panther was going to happen in one of several ways. The first might be the result of good old-fashioned detective and forensic work. Every effort was made to try to source the items found in the car and in the drainage shaft back to the manufacturers or retailers in the hopes that someone might remember selling an item to a particular customer they could still describe. But time and time again the police were able to get so far and then hit a wall, often because the Panther had covered his tracks with a false name and address for at least the past three years. Men who'd worked in the construction of the drainage shaft system were interviewed, but these ran into thousands and no answer was reached.

The pair of Zeiss binoculars found abandoned in the grass near the shaft entrance involved in the abortive drop could only be singled down to a batch sold in 1972. This told the police that the Panther had been planning the operation for at least three years, a fact supported by the meticulous duplication of all the kit found in the car and then down in the drainage shaft, and the equipment that had to be bought again after the discovery of the Ford van in the Kidsgrove area before Christmas. Even at that stage, the guarantee on the binoculars had been filled out with a false name and address. A sleeping bag bore a handwritten price tag and some initials on a label, but no one could remember writing the price tag and the initials turned out to be those of a quality controller in the factory.

The second hope was that someone in the kidnapper's family would find their conscience overcame their sense of loyalty. The feeling was that the kidnapper had a family, or at least a wife or girlfriend, based on some of the sightings of his vehicles. The public had reacted well with information, and this included the criminal fraternity who didn't like the crime, the kidnapper or the presence of so many police involved in the search. One enterprising newspaper came up with a quiz asking its readers if they knew anyone fitting the description of the kidnapper, and if so had he been away from home a lot, especially at night, and shouldn't they be examining their consciences and coming forward now?

It must have been tempting for the police or newspapers to suggest to the public that if friends or family didn't come forward then they might be the next ones. But this was not a pressure anyone would want to put on a family. One case that comes to mind is the girlfriend of John George Haigh, the Acid Baths Murderer: she said later in life that if he'd suspected she ever knew about his killing any of his six victims then she would have been number seven.

Whatever reluctance there might be on the part of family of the kidnapper, there was also a motive on the part of complete strangers not to come forward with information that might have been valuable. Many of the pieces of equipment scattered around Bathpool Park – the Thermos flasks, tape recorders and binoculars – would have alerted the police if they had been brought in at once by those who found them. Instead, they seem to have taken them home and made sure they stayed hidden in a drawer.

One of the children who found the sugar buns wrapped in cellophane near the shaft entrance recalled later that the buns appeared to be 'soft', and therefore fresh, at the time. Many of us would have done exactly the same as them, especially if we were only schoolchildren, but the fact remains that some of the findings, if reported immediately, might have accelerated the investigation.

The same applied to the courting couples in the park on the night of the abortive drop. At least two other couples were seen in the area besides Peter Shorto and his girlfriend, but they decided to remain anonymous for reasons best known to themselves.

The other reason the Panther might yet be caught was that he would still be short of money and might return to petty crime just to keep up an income. After all, the big payday hadn't happened. What looked like at least three years' work and preparation had come to nothing, so why not return to the potboilers, the post-office raids that had proved successful even if not very lucrative? The chances were that the Panther would mess up one of the robberies now, especially as he'd blown the big one and perhaps lost some confidence. He needed to keep his hand in, like the boxer who'd lost a prizefight having to return to the ring and work his way back up.

All this continually went through Donald Neilson's mind in the weeks and months after the kidnapping. This was worse than the previous biggest disaster of his life so far, failing the basic training course in the army and having to do it again when everyone else had passed. That was a public humiliation, and so would this episode be, if he was caught. But Donald Neilson wasn't a quitter, he told himself. He'd come back to take the course again and passed and been able to join his colleagues fighting out in Aden. In the same way he'd be back to try again. He kept going over in his mind how he could improve things: make the handover less complicated, find a family who wouldn't run off to the police and put a daughter's safety at risk instead of paying the ransom – and perhaps next time ask for more money.

Meanwhile, it was important to keep fit. He kept up his route marches, carrying a haversack with provisions for a night or two sleeping rough in the countryside, with flasks of soup and sugar buns to keep up the sugar levels. Being so fit had been a real advantage in the post office raids, when you could park the car some distance from each post office and disappear into the night.

It wasn't hard to see where this obsession with fitness and survival had come from. On 6 January 1955 Donald Neilson was conscripted into the army for two years' national service. While for many young men at this age national service was a little more than an unwelcome interruption to an apprenticeship or university, for Neilson it was the introduction to a world of excitement, guns and learning how to survive in difficult or hostile environments. It was the land of the living after the deadness of a school where he was bullied and a home where his mother died when he was 10 and his father would clobber him if he misbehaved. To make matters worse he was short, only 5ft 4in tall, and cursed with the surname of Nappey, a name guaranteed to give you years of persecution at school. Even his apprenticeships as a joiner and carpenter had failed. Now he became a lance corporal in the King's Own Yorkshire Light Infantry, handling .303 rifles and Bren guns, going on exercises where you survived on meagre rations and lived off the land for food and shelter. He even had to learn to walk again in order to survive gruelling route marches and assault courses, swinging his arms in a light infantry style that he took back into civilian life.

But even basic training did not go smoothly because, not to put a finer point on it, Neilson was not very good at it. He failed the ten-week course and had to take it again – he was 'back-squadded', something rare in recruits and surprising and demoralising for one so keen. He excused himself by saying he was enjoying life so much on the course that he deliberately failed the Bren gun section, but his incompetence was witnessed by his fellow recruits and his colleagues on active service. It surprised them later when they heard that it was 'Don' who'd become the Black Panther using military techniques he'd had such trouble mastering in his two years in the army.

When he successfully completed his training he was so proud to be in the army that he wore his battledress for his wedding, after which he was shipped out to Kenya to fight the Mau Mau terrorists in what was still a British colony. This was tough work in swamps and forests, living on rations supplemented by what they could take off the land. But there's little doubt this first six months of active service did much to mould Neilson's later life. They depended on self-sufficiency and a short-barrelled jungle .303 rifle, not unlike the sawn-off shotgun he armed himself with later. Each man was issued with fifty rounds of ammunition that he wore in a belt around the waist, like the belt he was wearing when eventually arrested.

But after the grimness of training in grey Yorkshire barracks, Kenya was a paradise of colour and mountain scenery, moving in forests where self-sufficiency wasn't difficult in the presence of plentiful game under a blue sky and trout in clear mountain streams. Next came Aden for six months, less pleasant in the heat and flies, and then Cyprus facing EOKA terrorists, with a terrain similar to Kenya. Cyprus showed Neilson how terrorists could live in caves with a cache of guns, food, maps and everything else needed for survival, not dissimilar to the caves of Dudley and the drainage shafts of Bathpool Park.

And so it was quite natural, for Neilson at least, to carry this life on when he was demobilised from the army after his two years of wearing army boots and camouflage jacket, driving a jeep and walking the light infantry step with a swing of the arms and quick, short pace. The family photo albums showed him, Irene and Kathryn on imaginary military manoeuvres in local woods, with 'Captain' Neilson directing, pointing to maps in the style of modern dictators in a photo opportunity, his wife playing the role of corpse in the smouldering wreck of another abandoned jeep they'd found, and Kathryn emerging from the undergrowth to hurl a stick grenade at the team.

18

When faced with the record of a serial killer like Donald Neilson the temptation is always to look for a cause. What sort of upbringing did he have? Was the family strapped for money? Did he get in with the wrong crowd? Did he have some sort of psychological problems, even if he wasn't insane, or was it simply pure evil? Did he enjoy the support of his family even if they weren't complicit in his crimes?

He was born as Donald Nappey in Morley, near Bradford, on 1 August 1936. His parents were both mill workers and lived in a one-up one-down terraced house overlooked by a mill in Morley. Donald was 4 when his sister was born and by this time the Second World War had started with all the privations brought by war, especially if one was living in reduced means anyway.

With a name like Nappey it wasn't difficult to guess that he would be bullied and teased at school, a situation made no happier because he was short. This in turn led to him having few real friends at school, and even the consolation of a stable and loving home came to an end when his mother died when he was only 10 years old. The bottom fell out of his world. He'd loved his mother and he, in turn, was the apple of her eye. She died of breast cancer after a long illness in the harsh winter of 1947.

It didn't take long for the young Donald to react and shortly after his mother's death he broke into the local Co-op and was caught. Although he got off with a ticking-off and warning from the police, it was his first venture into crime, a crime he regretted for getting caught rather than doing wrong.

Otherwise, Donald rallied to living in a household without a mother for him and a wife for his father, taking over responsibility for household chores, doing the shopping, cleaning, washing and even the cooking after lessons from his granny. There were housekeepers appointed by his father, but when it looked as if he might be intending to marry again and replace someone who in Donald's heart was irreplaceable, Donald decided it was time to leave home.

His new home was lodgings with a family who used to be neighbours. He had now left school and become an apprentice joiner, a hard worker but shy and withdrawn. He didn't smoke and he didn't drink, and this didn't make him many new friends and left him isolated. His one consolation and means to independence was his motorbike, which he could barely afford after leaving two apprenticeships in only twelve months. It wasn't the quality of his work, and he never shirked hard work or refused overtime: it was simply that he didn't fit in or thought that he was being exploited by his employer. Even the son of the family in lodgings, with whom he shared a bedroom for two or three years, felt he never really got to know him. He thought Donald was always trying to prove himself by doing daredevil acts on his bike or jumping off high walls. He thought Donald felt himself rejected after his mother's death, although in the lodgings he was treated just like any other member of the family.

But the independence given to him by his motorbike paid off in allowing him to go to local dances. He was a good dancer and met his future wife, Irene Tate, at 19 two years older than him, at a dance at Bradford Textile Hall, and they were married at St Paul's parish church on 30 April 1955. They made a good-looking couple, Irene in a white wedding dress and Donald in army battledress with a white carnation in his buttonhole. He'd only been in the army at this stage for four months and was on forty-eight hours' compassionate leave before being sent out to Kenya. None of the family were invited, not even Irene's mother and sister, and it wasn't for another four months that they found out about the wedding. The two witnesses at the ceremony were Donald's aunt and uncle, and they'd only been invited the day before. They only saw him about once more after the wedding.

When Donald came out of the army after his two-year stint of national service the couple couldn't get a house of their own and so they lodged with Irene's eldest sister. During the three years they were there Kathryn was born, on 12 January 1960. Now with a baby the family moved into a house in Grangefield Avenue, Bradford, that Donald started altering straight away with the conversion of the attic space into bedrooms.

But work continued to be a problem for Donald, and he decided to become a door-to-door-salesman. He abandoned this in 1962 because, once again, he couldn't fit into a team working under a boss. The answer was to try to be self-employed, but making a profit out of waste paper, salvaging metal stripped from scrap vehicles and window cleaning was difficult. In 1965 he bought a Morris Oxford car and used this for three years for private hire, but even here he was cursed with not being able to fit in and work in a pool of drivers, and the traditional rivalry between private car hire drivers and licensed taxis.

Probably with a young daughter approaching school age and the memories of the taunting he received at school and in the army, Donald decided to rid himself of the name Nappey once and for all and become Neilson instead. He didn't look far for a suitable name and took that of the former proprietor of the car hire business he had just closed. Armed with a new name and new hope, he went back into the joinery business, even taking on small house extensions and employing others to work for him. Another of his projects was erecting garden sheds that he constructed in the back garden and then put on a garage forecourt for display and sale. After working all the hours of daylight possible during the week, he then worked on the petrol pumps at weekends to pay the rent for displaying his sheds on the forecourt. It was ceaseless work that presented him with continual cash flow problems.

In a further attempt to raise an income, Donald decided to convert parts of the house into flatlets, putting in washbasins with hot and cold water himself. It was cramped, but provided accommodation for two single women and a married couple. One of the women who babysat for them noticed Donald and Irene often went out late at 10 or 10.30 p.m. and came back late without ever saying where they'd been. Otherwise, no family or friends visited the house, not even friends of Kathryn's.

Neighbours saw little of the couple, only if Donald appeared to carry out repairs on the house, something he did with considerable bravery when, for example, fixing roof tiles during a gale. But he remained secretive, never telling anyone where he went if he was working away, wearing army uniform and walking with the familiar military swing of the arms and spring in the step and apparently, on the rare occasions a neighbour got into the house to witness it, keeping the place in a disorganised mess.

In 1975, after the kidnapping, Donald decided to sell Grangefield Avenue. This might have been for several reasons. Over the years Donald had become less and less enchanted with his immigrant neighbours who had created an Asian community on what was, in essence, a huge traffic roundabout in Grangefield Avenue. The Neilsons' next-door neighbour had sold his house to an Asian family who turned up with a suitcase full of money to pay for it. Donald's frustration was his apparent inability to make any money while these people could float in with ready cash. It was interesting that after his arrest the police were surprised that many living in the street were unaware of the Neilsons and had never heard of the Black Panther.

The other reason for moving house might well have been that in the last few years he had murdered four people, to include Lesley Whittle in January that year. Moving to Pudsey, a town between Bradford and Leeds, would put a bit of distance between these crimes and anyone trying to come after him. But of course there was the problem of the arsenal of weapons that was carefully hidden away in Grangefield Avenue, together with the campaign maps and the rest of the paraphernalia used to carry out the raids. In the short term, it meant estate agents coming around the house to make a valuation, followed by prospective purchasers. In the end, Neilson decided to market the house himself without using agents, and when it came to buyers looking around he would try to avoid his office on the second floor completely by saying it was merely a storeroom, or if they insisted on looking he would open the door in only the swiftest of inspections. Not the best way to try to sell a house and he probably left the buyers wondering exactly what he had to hide and, if it came to it, why he would flatly refuse to let anyone look into the attic space above the room.

Like so many plans made by Donald Neilson in his lifetime, it all came to nothing when he couldn't find the money to buy the house they'd found in Pudsey. Had they gone through with the sale and purchase, the intriguing question remains how Neilson would have transferred the arsenal to the new house without arousing suspicion and where he would have stored it all in a house not yet adapted to Panther specifications.

Whichever house the Neilsons were living in, life for Kathryn remained grim for a girl in her teenage years. If friends came to the house they were only allowed into Kathryn's bedroom, which probably wasn't hugely surprising as the rest of the house was taken over by her father's workroom and campaign office on the ground floor and inner sanctum on the second floor, where no one was allowed to enter. But for Kathryn it was one-way traffic: friends could come in but she wasn't allowed out. To say her father was possessive was an understatement and a terrible irony in view of the way he treated Lesley Whittle, who was only a year older than Kathryn. Donald had suggested that Kathryn come and work for him once she'd left school at the age of 15, but not surprisingly this was not an idea that appealed to her.

A scheme was worked out whereby Kathryn's aunt would have her over to stay once a week and that would give Kathryn the chance to get out for a Friday evening with her cousin and stay the night with them. When Donald found out by reading her diary after one of his 'inspections' of her bedroom he was furious. This was blatantly disobeying orders and her punishment was solitary confinement in her bedroom for the full six weeks of the summer holidays, having to take her meals in her room brought up by her mother, with whom she was not allowed to speak. To keep her fit and mindful of her lack of discipline, she had to wash paintwork in the house, strip wallpaper and, in the most sadistic punishment of all, move bricks from one side of the backyard to another and then move them back again.

Keeping fit was extended to a slightly more humanitarian side when she was allowed to accompany her father swimming at the local baths, or go on runs with him through the local woods. Then there were the family military exercises on local scrubland with Donald recreating the exercises he carried out while in the army and keeping in shape for his current campaigns. They would all dress in fatigues or battledress and be fully briefed by 'Captain' Neilson before they went out on manoeuvres.

Part of Neilson's obsession with his daughter's protection must have been knowing what he had in mind for a member of the Whittle family, that he would soon be chaining them by the neck to a ladder some 60ft below ground in the cold and dark. This was something that was never going to happen to his own daughter. He really loved Kathryn, she represented innocence and total obedience in a world that he never really understood and that treated him as a failure.

The thing that worried Neilson more now was the spate of copycat kidnappings since Lesley Whittle, and these had all been unsuccessful, with the kidnappers caught and the money returned. This was giving the police experience in the crime, and if he did have another try they would be that much more experienced. He had to remind himself of one thing – he hadn't been caught. As the days, weeks and then months went by there still hadn't come the knock on the door, or the smash of glass in the middle of the night with no time to grab the gun before they were in the house and on him. There was no sign of the police and it was now December and nearly a year after he'd gone into the Whittle household and taken the girl.

He felt more relaxed now, able to go out into the streets without fear of being recognised; so much so that he even felt confident enough to have another go at a post office raid and make sure he hadn't lost his touch. He reminded himself he was the professional and they were the amateurs. He'd bought a new car now, had a target premises in mind and had even done some snooping in the area, Mansfield this time, to make a bit of a change. He got out a few of the old tools, to include the shotgun, and put them in his holdall.

Just be his luck if on the first outing back on the job he got picked up …

And, sure enough, this was just what happened.

19

At 10.40 p.m. on the evening of Thursday, 11 December 1975, two young police constables were on routine duty in their panda car in Mansfield Woodhouse. They were parked in Stainforth Road facing the main A60 Walsall to Worksop road a few yards away, when a short, wiry figure dressed in dark clothes and carrying a bag walked across their view along the far side of the main road. He walked quickly with a spring in his step.

The police officers were Tony White and Stuart Mackenzie. 'Worth a look?' asked Mackenzie. White nodded. The times that they'd carried out a routine check like this probably ran into the hundreds, but there was something furtive, even slightly comical, with this one as he scurried along the pavement taking short, springy paces, swinging his left arm and clutching the holdall in the other.

Mackenzie started the engine and they drew out into the main road, slowing down again as they drew parallel with their man. White wound down the window. 'Good evening, sir,' he said. 'At this time of night we always check out strangers. Would you mind telling us your name, address, and where you have been?'

The man slowed without coming to a halt. He kept looking straight ahead without wanting to look down at the car. 'I'm coming back from work,' he said.

'Where's that?' asked White.

'I'm a lorry driver.' Both the man and the car had now come to a halt.

'Then would you please give me your name and address,' asked White.

The man paused for a while before answering, as if he was thinking hard about it. 'My name is John Moxson.'

White pinned a notepad to his clipboard and started writing. 'I see, sir. And date of birth.'

Again there was a wait while the man martialled the details in his head. 'I was born on 30 January 1937.'

'And place of birth, please.'

Slightly less of a pause this time. 'I was born at Chapel-en-le-Frith.'

This was a small town in Derbyshire about an hour away, and White wrote it down.

The man leaned forward. 'Don't move!' he barked, and as he did so he put his hand into the holdall and pulled out a double-barrelled shotgun. 'In the back,' he ordered White, who was sitting in the passenger seat. White started to open his door to get into the back when the man said, 'No time for that. Climb over the seat.' White did as he was told and the man took his place in the front passenger seat. He turned to Mackenzie and poked the barrels of the gun into his side below the armpit. 'Right,' he said. 'Drive.'

'Where to?' asked Mackenzie.

'Just drive,' was the reply.

As the car drew off Mackenzie asked again where he should drive to. The man kept staring straight at Mackenzie and wasn't going to be fooled into taking his eyes off him and on to the road. 'Take it easy and drive normally. Any tricks and you're both dead,' he said.

They drove for a while, until the man said, 'Put that police sign on the roof out.' Mackenzie did what he was told and switched the sign off. Both police officers held their breath, waiting for the opportunity when their captor might just lose concentration for a split second and look out of the window to see where they were going. They could almost hear him thinking what he was going to do next and where he was going to do it.

'Any tricks and you've had it,' he repeated. He was breathing hard and his breath smelt of tea. Suddenly he said, as if he'd been rehearsing the request in his mind, 'Can you take me to Blidworth?'

'Yes sir, certainly sir,' the officers replied in unison.

Mackenzie drove on a short distance and when he came to the junction with Hartley Avenue asked if it was all right to turn around. He was told it was, and making the turn he drove back the way they had come, as far as the junction with the Four Ways pub where Mackenzie turned left. After this change of direction the tension was reduced slightly. Still without moving his head the man listened to the crackle of the car radio. 'Can they hear us on that?' he asked.

Mackenzie had anticipated he might ask and was ready with an answer. 'If they call us we'll have to answer, sir, otherwise they'll become suspicious and set up roadblocks.'

'They've had me in once and I'm not going back again,' the man replied grimly.

The journey then settled into an uneasy calm. The two officers desperately tried to engage the man in some sort of conversation, even though it was banal comments about the condition of the panda car or their families. Anything just to break down the barrier between them and let him know they had families too and would like to live long enough to see them again.

Meanwhile two big questions stayed firmly at the front of their minds. Who had they caught and what was he going to do with them? It wasn't as if they'd caught him in the middle of committing a crime. If he was a lorry driver, where was his lorry and why was he footing it up a main road? He'd been brought in by the police for something before and he was self-assured, as if he knew what he was doing. They'd both got a look at his eyes when he pulled the gun and got into the car and the man wasn't just angry, he was livid. 'Oh God,' thought Mackenzie – and the thought wasn't far behind in White's mind – they hadn't caught the Black Panther? They'd seen the posters and he was the right height, ill-kempt, and thin-faced. They knew he'd killed three sub-postmasters, attacked a security man and kidnapped the girl. Now it was their turn, unless they did something quickly.

As Mackenzie kept the half-hearted conversation afloat, and toyed with the idea that this was the Panther, the fact that he was being asked to go to Blidworth suddenly took on new significance. The drive would be all countryside with plenty of opportunity for him to shoot them and abandon the car. The only built-up area they'd meet would be through Rainworth, and although it was getting on for eleven now there was at least the probability that people would be around coming back from the pub or getting takeaways.

It was their only chance.

Any real hope that they might be calming the man in the passenger seat was lost when he asked, 'I want to tie you up. Do you have any rope?'

'No, afraid not, sir,' said Mackenzie.

'There might be,' said White from the back more hopefully, 'but I'll have to move around a bit to find it. Is that all right?'

'Yes, but no tricks or he'll get it,' said the man, prodding the barrel into Mackenzie's ribs.

White pretended to rummage around in the back seat and floor looking for rope or anything else that might serve to tie them up. All the while he kept a careful eye on the gun just in case it moved from Mackenzie's armpit. As they entered the village of Rainworth, Mackenzie noticed two things. Firstly there were people milling around the chip shop now the pubs were closing. And secondly, coming up ahead of them, was a fork in the road. 'Which way?' he asked, leaning forward in his seat to peer out of the windscreen.

For the first time, the Panther looked up and tried to remember which the right way was. It was enough. He lost his concentration and lowered the gun on to Mackenzie's lap. Immediately White lunged at the gun and Mackenzie stamped on the brakes. White shouted, 'Get him!'

He didn't need telling twice. As the car slid to a halt Mackenzie was able to take his hands off the wheel and join the struggle, and between them they forced the gun up to the roof, where it went off with a shattering explosion and blew a large hole in the roof. 'He's shot me!' shouted White.

Mackenzie half fell, half struggled out of the car and shouted at the customers outside the chip shop, 'For God's sake help us. We've a man with a shotgun!' He ran around to the passenger door and managed to put their assailant into an armlock and drag him out on to the pavement, where he pushed him face down with a knee on his neck. By this time customers from the shop had run over to help and Mackenzie managed to fish out a pair of handcuffs, which he gave to someone to put on their prisoner. They dragged him over to a set of railings near the shop and with another set of handcuffs chained him to railings.

The hunt was over. The quarry was at bay.

The Panther now stood quietly at the railings, his head bowed, his face cut and already bruising from the efforts by both the public and the two police officers to subdue him. His pursuers stood a few feet away, looking at him, not sure what they'd caught.

PC White brought over the shotgun from the car and gave it to Mackenzie. 'I must phone for assistance,' he said, and holding up the shotgun to the onlookers added, 'Could one of you kindly take this for me?' A local lady, Mrs Rosaline Palmer, stepped forward from the crowd, anxious to do her bit. 'I'll put it back in the car for you. Just to keep it safe,' she said, and carrying the weapon carefully with two hands took it back over to the car and propped it up in the passenger seat, still warm and still loaded.

After police assistance arrived and Neilson was taken away, Mackenzie walked over to the panda car. He looked at the hole blown in the roof of the car, and the shotgun sitting innocently in the front seat. His ears were still ringing from the shot and a pain started in his left ear. Suddenly he realised how different the scene might have looked, he and White reduced to two corpses in or beside their abandoned car out in the countryside somewhere, the gun and their attacker gone, and a manhunt under way.

He picked up the gun uncertainly, his hands shaking. A calm voice he didn't recognise asked behind him, 'Why don't you let me have that, officer? I was in the services and I think it's best we unload it.' Mackenzie let him take the gun, break it and take out the two cartridges, one empty and the other still live.

20

With Neilson safely transferred to a cell in Mansfield Police Station, stripped and wrapped in a blanket and his fingerprints taken, the head of Mansfield CID, Detective Superintendent John McNaught, was brought in from home to take a look at what they'd caught.

By coincidence he probably knew more about the Black Panther than anyone in the police force, and it didn't take him long after being confronted by the arsenal removed from their prisoner to guess this was either the Black Panther himself or someone in the same league trying to operate like him. The collection, removed from him and arranged on a couple of tables like exhibits in Scotland Yard's Black Museum, included a choice of hoods, a shotgun and ammunition belt of cartridges, torches and knives. Much of the equipment was in duplicate, to include two watches, knives, even two pairs of gloves and two reels of sticking plaster, presumably to bind or gag his victims. The most subtle were two razor blades, one hidden inside a cigarette lighter case and the other sewn into his jacket. Tied to his cartridge belt was a block of something wrapped in black plastic that looked and felt suspiciously like explosives, but forensics later analysed this as a high-protein biscuit in case Neilson needed to hole up somewhere and avoid capture.

If he wanted to do a survey into his next target there was a pair of binoculars around his neck, a compass and an Ordnance Survey map of Nottinghamshire. An implement for boring holes in metal was recognised as the tool used in the robberies for drilling into window frames – a tool that would probably have remained unrecognised if the police weren't now aware of the Black Panther's modus operandi.

McNaught had attended the scene in 1967 when the Woodfield Road sub-post office had been raided, later at Berry Hill Lane, and then other raids as they became a pattern. He saw Neilson in his office still wrapped in his blanket and now handcuffed to an arm of his chair. His right eye was turning into a real shiner, his nose had stopped bleeding and there were cuts to his face left by the public helping out with the arrest in Rainworth.

Lying on McNaught's desk was an artist's impression of 'Britain's Most Wanted'. He held it up and looked from the prisoner to the sketch and back again. 'A man wearing a hood is wanted for some serious offences in various parts of the country. I suspect you are that man,' he said.

'Not true,' came the reply in pidgin English. 'I no shoot anybody.'

McNaught suggested he was sufficiently armed to shoot anybody, including the two police officers.

'I would shoot dog but no policeman. I no Black Panther. When Black Panther work, he shoots to kill,' was the indignant reply.

McNaught left off the question of the Black Panther, or even what his real name was, and asked why he requested the police officers take him to Blidworth, aware that this was well into Forestry Commission land and the ideal place to shoot the officers and make a run for it. He asked why he'd fired the shotgun in the car, but got the reply that this was an accident. He got a little further when he asked Neilson where he had been going when he was arrested in Woodhouse, and here Neilson felt he hadn't much to lose by replying that he was looking for premises to burgle.

Two things had already become obvious in this questioning. The first was the suspect's inability to answer questions in less than ten or fifteen minutes, presumably to give himself time to calculate to avoid incriminating himself. The second was this odd clipped accent that McNaught first took as a European accent, and then Welsh.

By the following morning no name had been established beyond 'John Moxson', and so McNaught, having already sent the fingerprints off to Scotland Yard, asked someone in his local team to compare them with a photograph of the half print they'd been able to copy from the notebook in the drainage shaft at Bathpool. They matched. It looked as if they'd got their man.

But still they couldn't get a real name out of him, or whether or not he was the Black Panther. In the end the head of Nottinghamshire CID, Detective Chief Superintendent Roy Readwin, locked himself in the cell with 'Mr Moxson' and subtly questioned him for two hours on the Friday evening, alone and without it looking like an interrogation.

The breakthrough came with a question that implied that he might not be up to these crimes alone. Readwin asked whether not giving his real name was trying to protect an accomplice.

'I always work alone,' replied the suspect, unhappy at the suggestion. 'If I am the Black Panther and they charge me with four murders, it is better my family do not know. I will just disappear from sight behind bars for ever.'

Readwin reminded him that this wouldn't be possible if they had to publish photos on television and in the newspapers. That changed things.

'If I tell you my name and address will you get in touch with my wife?' asked his suspect. When this was agreed, the answer came at last. 'My name is Donald Neilson. I live in Leeds Road, Bradford,' and he gave a telephone number for his wife, insisting on shaking hands with Readwin to make it a deal.

A raiding party was then immediately dispatched to Bradford, but was unable to find the Neilson household in Leeds Road. The mystery was solved by local police who traced the house to its correct address in Grangefield Avenue. This was not because Neilson was trying a last attempt at confusing the police, but because the locals called Grangefield Avenue the 'Leeds Road' simply because it was on the main road out of Bradford to Leeds.

The question of liaison, or lack of it, between the various police forces came up in the Neilson case. If local police could solve a question of an address in Bradford in moments, how much time could have been saved by local police helping Ronald Whittle find Kidsgrove Post Office and the correct car park in Bathpool Park in Neilson's directions?

The police party finally arrived at the house in Grangefield Avenue and, after surrounding the house, rang the bell. A woman in a dressing gown opened the door a few inches and peered out.

'Mrs Neilson?'

The woman nodded.

'We are police officers and here in connection with your husband's arrest in Mansfield. May we come in?'

Mrs Neilson's face was impassive. This was probably the call she'd half-expected for years, and watching the television that evening she had perhaps guessed that it was Donald being held. 'Is he all right?' she asked.

With all the hubbub going on, Kathryn came down from her bedroom. The two women were escorted back upstairs by two female officers to get dressed and then accompany the search team as they went through the house room by room, so that there was no possibility of anyone later saying evidence had been planted.

The lounge was the first room to be searched, converted by Neilson into an operations room, with notes on various premises dotted around Mansfield that might make suitable targets for burglaries, including an exercise book of sketches, road maps and escape routes. Some of the notes detailed idiosyncrasies of the target premises, such as when the lights went out at night or where dogs barked nearby. One of the target premises turned out to be a pub very near where the two officers originally picked up Neilson in Mansfield Woodhouse.

Next was the dining room which had been converted into a workshop for Neilson's carpentry business, complete with tools, pieces of wood and work benches. In a sideboard, instead of what you might expect in the way of glasses or crockery ready to be used in the dining room, was a heavy object wrapped in a T-shirt and thrust to the back of a drawer.

Inspector Bevington carefully unwrapped the parcel, expecting a gun or something similar that Neilson obviously wanted hidden – but instead found a 6in black ceramic model of a panther. Mrs Neilson explained that her husband had bought the model black panther for Kathryn as a present while they were on holiday in Blackpool two years ago, and that it had stood on the sideboard until her husband took it down and put it in the back of the drawer. Neilson was to say later that he admired the panther for its speed, skill, strength and stealth. It was its stealth that particularly impressed him.

The search became interesting again on the second floor when the detectives found a locked door across the corridor from the master bedroom. Irene Neilson, who was still accompanying the police team, announced she couldn't open the door because she hadn't got a key and had never been given a key because this was 'his room'.

The door was forced to reveal what quickly became obvious as the Panther's lair. For someone who didn't know Donald Neilson or anything about the household, looking around at the chaos in this room – the clothes hanging out of drawers, the backpacks and maps, the masks and wigs – that person could be forgiven for thinking the room belonged to an adolescent who was fond of dressing up and going for long hikes in the countryside, where he occasionally camped out for periods, cooking and surviving on his own, with dreams one day of joining the army and doing the real thing once he'd grown up a bit first and put his life in order.

But, for the police now holding the suspected Black Panther, the room was an Aladdin's cave of evidence against him: masks that had been used in the various raids; a tape recorder similar to the one used in the kidnapping; a DYMO tape punch to print out the directions in the ransom drops; and U-bolts similar to those used to clamp the ligatures around Lesley's neck and the ladder in the shaft.

More searchers were brought into the house first thing in the morning and they found newspaper cuttings reporting the Black Panther activities along with his identikit picture. There was also a do-it-yourself car registration kit with a few made-up plates that had never been used.

But that wasn't the end of it. There was a small inspection hatch leading into the roof space above the attic room, and here the team found a double-barrelled shotgun and a large biscuit tin with hundreds of rounds of different types of ammunition. Bizarrely, perhaps in case the Panther had found himself run to earth without guns or ammunition, there were two crossbows. There were several haversacks, one containing over 800 vehicle ignition keys. Finally, from this cache they extracted a .22 rifle in a leather case from a cavity wall. From under the floor in the attic room came jemmies, a leather cosh and a .22 repeater rifle.

A bunch of nine keys told the police a little more about how Neilson moved around the Midlands. Three related to a motorcycle that explained the helmet and leathers found in his room, but not the absence of a motorbike – Neilson said later he must have left it somewhere in a car park on the outskirts of Birmingham. The other six keys belonged to lock-up garages around Birmingham and Northampton, providing a network of supply bases for vehicles or safe storage for stolen property. At one stage Neilson had thought he might use one of the garages as a prison cell for his kidnap victims.

But first the investigation team had to try to move things beyond Neilson simply giving them his name and address, and for this Commander John Morrison and two of his senior officers set themselves up in Kidsgrove Police Station in the early hours of Saturday, 13 December. They rolled up their sleeves, made the tea and prepared to sit it out for as long as it took for Neilson to stop using his squeaky pidgin English and explain how he'd taken matters from robbing sub-post offices to kidnap and murder.

Meanwhile, on the same Saturday morning over at Grangefield Avenue, after the police photographers had been through the house recording the scene in every room, nook and cranny, Detective Inspector Bevington looked through a pile of ashes in the fireplace in the lounge. There were the remains of a considerable number of pieces of paper, and the fire had been recent and thorough, leaving little trace of what had actually been burned. But, reaching up into the chimney, he found a single postal order, singed at the edges but intact and legible. Someone in the last couple of days had made a bonfire of dozens, if not hundreds, of postal orders.

21

For Irene and Kathryn, Donald's arrest came as something of a relief, although Irene would face charges in connection with the cashing of the postal orders, and say she was in an abusive marriage where she had little choice but to obey the orders of her husband. Kathryn, at the time of the abduction, was only six months younger than Lesley Whittle. One has only to guess what was going through her mind as her father's trial proceeded and she heard how he had removed a girl her age from her bed in the middle of the night and imprisoned her at the bottom of a drainage shaft, naked in a sleeping bag, while he cavorted around the countryside trying to collect a bag of cash.

In fact, we don't have to guess what was going through her mind, because at the end of the trial Kathryn recorded exactly what she felt about her father and had felt about him as she entered her teenage years. She said she wouldn't remember him as a loving father, but as a monster in her home. Only she and her mother knew the man who became the Black Panther and how for years he made life hell for her with his bullying. She said that at the time of his arrest she was on the point of running away from home, just as soon as she'd finished her GCE exams. Now that he was in gaol it was if a great black cloud had been lifted because most times on returning home she'd have to ask what sort of mood her father was in and if it was a bad mood, which it most often was, she went straight up to her room to avoid him.

She thought one of the problems was that he really wanted a son rather than a daughter, and so when she would rather have been playing in the park with her friends, he'd wanted her playing war games with her parents in the local woods. When she asked for a Sindy doll for Christmas, he gave her an Action Man complete with machine gun and sleeping bag. On another occasion he gave her a complete battlefield with soldiers he'd made from papier mâché and insisted on playing a war game that could last five hours.

There were a couple of occasions demonstrating the relatively minor incidents that could throw Donald Neilson into a rage. When he was trying to teach Kathryn as a child how to tell the time, he suddenly lost his patience and threw the clock across the room. The other was following Neilson's buying the Champ vehicle he used for his war games with the family in the woods. He was so proud of the machine that he went on a Champs owners' rally, only to make a spectacle of himself by taking a shortcut through a field and getting bogged down in the middle. Other members of the rally had to come and help push him out, leaving him speechless with rage at being made to look such a fool. The lance corporal who wanted to look like a general was being made to look like a lance corporal, and that's what he couldn't tolerate.

It was the volatility of her father's moods and trying avoid anything that would trigger a mood that posed the problems for Kathryn. Despite the fact that he missed the army and fantasised about it so much, he never contemplated rejoining it or even the territorials. It was the 'Walter Mitty' world that attracted him, a world where he wasn't judged and where he couldn't fail. His various civilian moneymaking schemes of door-to-door salesman, running a taxi, window cleaning and carpentry had all failed.

But his military operations in planning and executing crimes were, in his eyes, a success, in that he'd always got away even if they hadn't made him much money.

Kathryn could see her father's mental state deteriorating in the last two years before his arrest. It wasn't just the moods, it was the sitting on the sofa at home and brooding, staring into space, or suddenly coming to and snapping some random question at Kathryn, or presumably Irene as well, and then swearing at them in the most abusive terms if they got the answer wrong. Then there was the obsession with having a clean fork at mealtimes, with the fork having to be cleaned several times before being acceptable; or food that hadn't been cooked correctly; or tea that was too hot.

For someone who was becoming increasingly violent in his criminal life and did not show any remorse for his victims, it was a surprise to find Neilson had a dislike for anything sad in films and books, and would even shed a tear if he thought no one was looking.

Inevitably reports of the Black Panther crimes would come on to the television news in the Neilson household, watched with much interest by Donald. Anyone else in the room would be told to shut up while the news was on and his only comment would be that if anyone pointed a gun at a member of his family then he hoped that they would show a bit more sense than to try and fight back.

No one could say he didn't have a sense of humour. On one occasion, Irene came home to find Kathryn stretched out apparently unconscious on the sofa, her arm wrapped in bandages and covered in blood. Irene went into a panic and screamed for help, at which point Donald couldn't contain himself any longer and started laughing at what he saw as a particularly clever practical joke. Kathryn, who'd been primed to take part, burst into life and revealed the blood as tomato sauce.

This leaves the question of where both Kathryn and Irene thought Donald was in those last two years when he was away from the house so much, sometimes overnight or for a day or two. His excuse was that a friend had broken down somewhere and he was out to help him, or that it was a business trip and that he'd be working away. While some families might be suspicious and suspect an affair, Irene told Kathryn that he wasn't very interested in women, whatever that implied. Instead, the two women in his life breathed a sigh of relief when he left, unaware of what he was doing and caring even less. Kathryn would describe waiting five minutes to make sure he really had gone and hadn't forgotten anything, and then throwing herself on the sofa, shouting and laughing. Sometimes she'd scream just to release the tension.

Creating tension for other people was Donald Neilson's particular gift.

22

At nearly three o'clock the next morning, Commander John Morrison, head of Scotland Yard's murder squad, and two other senior police officers sat at a table in a police interview room with Donald Neilson. Neilson made a solitary figure with his black eye, bloody nose and cut face. He held a plastic cup of tea in one hand and, although he looked down at the table not wanting to look his captors in the eye, his head was no longer bowed.

If it hadn't been for the seniority of the officers interviewing him, Neilson might have passed for any Friday night casualty from a pub fight in for a few questions and then put in the cells for the night until he sobered up. But instead Commander Morrison and his colleagues now had their first chance to speak to the most wanted man in England who'd managed to escape them for the last ten months, a man they now knew had killed four times and nearly taken out a couple of police officers and a security guard as well. They'd read the reports and the witness statements and had wondered what they were going to find when they eventually caught him.

Morrison read him the caution and cleared his throat. 'Donald, you are at Kidsgrove Police Station.'

There was the faintest flicker of disbelief in Neilson's eyes asking why they were stating the obvious. But he supposed they had to say that. Anyway, he didn't mind being told the obvious. He didn't have to think.

'We are investigating the murder and kidnap of Lesley Whittle,' Morrison continued.

This was more difficult.

'Lesley Whittle was abducted from her home in Highley in Shropshire on 14 January this year in the early hours of the morning. Her body was found hanging at the foot of a shaft in Bathpool Park, Kidsgrove on 7 March. We have reason to believe that you can assist us with our enquiries,' Morrison continued in a matter-of-fact voice.

Now this was getting tricky. They weren't beating around the bush. Neilson hoped they might start with the arrest tonight and he could explain that he was planning a raid on a premises, but he hadn't decided where yet and he was sorry he jumped the police officers and he thought they'd done a great job in preventing a crime. Something like that. After all, no one had got hurt.

But this – coming straight out with the girl. They couldn't know about that. They were bluffing. After a period of fifteen minutes Neilson came up with his answer. 'No sir, not me sir, not Lesley Whittle,' he said, with the authority of a chess master checking the opponent's move.

Morrison looked at his two colleagues who had waited patiently for this answer. He turned to Neilson. 'Do you feel quite fit, Donald, or would you like a rest?' he asked. At this rate they were going to get through about four questions an hour.

Neilson wondered if this was a trick question, decided it wasn't and said, 'No, thank you, sir. I'm wide awake but you look a little tired.' Not a bad answer that, batted it straight back with a touch of humour.

'Very well, then,' said Morrison, taking a sip of his tea. 'Have you been to Highley, Donald?'

There it was again. Straight out of the blue. Well, he wasn't going to say yes, was he, if he'd never had anything to do with the girl? Highley was so small – if he'd said yes there could only be one conclusion. It wasn't as if he was being asked had he ever been to Wolverhampton or Bradford. He only took ten minutes to answer this one. 'No sir, not me sir.'

'Have you ever been to Bathpool Park then?'

Now this was less easy to deny, because Bathpool Park was a bit bigger than Highley and he might have visited the park with his wife and daughter. He tried to think if he'd ever visited the park before he'd gone there to stake it out, before all those wanderings and explorations. It gave him a headache just thinking about it. He reckoned they were still bluffing. Well, two could play at that. The answer came after twelve minutes. 'I not sure about this, sir,' he replied, abbreviating his answer into the sort of shorthand he used when confronting the enemy.

Morrison looked at his watch. This was getting worse than yes or no, this was becoming 'not sure'. He wondered if Neilson was suffering from some sort of amnesia after his bashing in the arrest. 'Would you like a cup of tea, Donald?' he asked, as if he was really asking what the matter was.

'Yes, please, sir,' replied Neilson, relieved at being asked something less tricky.

Tea was made and brought in on a tray. Morrison decided to ask the obvious. 'Why are you taking so long to answer the questions, Donald?'

This was another tricky one. Why didn't they just come out with a question that made it obvious they knew it was him, like something they found in the car or down the shaft? Then he might just give up and tell them everything. But instead they were teasing him. They knew the girl lived in Highley and they found her in Kidsgrove, but there was still the chance they couldn't connect it with him.

He was still thinking about all this after nine minutes. 'Do you understand what I'm asking you?' asked Morrison.

'Yes sir,' he replied.

'Well, why do you take so long to answer my questions?'

'I'm thinking, sir.'

'Are you feeling all right, then?'

'Perfectly well, sir.'

Detective Chief Superintendent Wright thought he might contribute to the questioning, just to give himself something to do. 'Do you want anything, Donald, anything more to eat or drink?'

'Another cup of tea, please, sir,' replied Neilson. His eye was hurting and the cuts around his face were beginning to irritate. His scalp felt like it was contracting. But a soldier would never admit to this while under interrogation. Don't show them your weakness otherwise they'll take advantage.

'Donald, if you're tired or unwell we can continue with this later on in the morning,' said Morrison.

'No, I all right, I need to think carefully. I need time to think.'

'That's understandable, Donald,' said Wright. 'This is a very serious matter, I want you to be sure you understand the questions clearly, if you are in any doubt about anything asked then you must say so. We are only trying to get to the truth.'

Neilson was asked if he wanted more time to collect his thoughts, and when he said he did Morrison changed the subject for a while. 'Well then, let's go into your background a bit because there's precious little we know about you as yet. You're a married man?'

'Yes sir.'

'Have you children?'

'Yes sir. I got girl.'

'How old is she?'

'About 16. What do you want to know about her for? What's that got to do with this?' Neilson then said he was 39, and had served in the army for a couple of years as a lance corporal in Aden, for which he said he'd had no special training.

The time was coming up to 4.30 a.m. and the three officers took a break after telling Neilson they'd be back shortly to resume their questions on Highley and Bathpool Park and Lesley Whittle.

When they came back after about three quarters of an hour, Morrison asked Neilson if he'd now had enough time to think. After he said he had had enough time he started to get distressed before any more questions could be put him. He started crying with his face down on the table, and then suddenly became quiet, remaining silent for twenty-five minutes.

They asked if he was all right, whether he was in any sort of pain, but he said he was all right and didn't need a doctor. They asked again if he'd been to Highley or Bathpool Park, and this time the answer was he didn't know because he'd been to lots of places, nor could he remember where he was in the early hours of 14 January because dates meant nothing to him.

Morrison said that, despite him not being able to recall whether he'd been to Highley or Bathpool Park, he fitted closely the description of the man they wished to speak to concerning the matter. 'Are you the person responsible for the kidnap and murder of Lesley Whittle?' asked Morrison.

Neilson started crying again, and then after a silence of eleven minutes said, 'No sir, not me, not murder the young girl.'

Morrison explained that it was their duty to put these questions to him.

'Yes sir, I know you got a job to do but it's all too distressing.'

With that they decided to let Neilson get some sleep and told him they would resume the interview later in the day. They gave him, in fact, eight-and-a-half hours to sleep and be fed, and when they all met again Neilson was cautioned again and reminded that he was there to answer questions about the murder of Lesley Whittle. Was there anything he wanted to say about the matter?

After ten minutes, he said, 'It's distressing.'

Morrison pointed out that for anyone not connected with the matter it was distressing, so why was he saying it was distressing?

'All of it, it's distressing,' Neilson repeated. He then admitted that he had visited both Highley and Bathpool once or twice, and had even gone down into the underground culvert at Bathpool after finding an open manhole last year. He was cagier about Dudley, on the defensive as to why he was being questioned about Dudley, but then admitted he had visited the zoo and knew the caves.

So Morrison returned to the main question and asked again if he had kidnapped and murdered Lesley Whittle. When again the question was met with silence Morrison repeated it, but this time adding that if he was saying he did commit the offence then did he have an accomplice?

Neilson immediately rose to the bait. 'Why do you have to bring an accomplice into it, why?' he asked petulantly.

'Because it's our duty to be thorough with such matters. Do you want to give us a straight yes or no?'

Now at last, after hours of patient questioning, of repeating a question here and going off on another topic there, after asking whether he was okay or would like a drink or food or even see a doctor, all the hard work paid off with the first crack in the ice.

'I didn't murder her,' said Neilson. 'I didn't even know who I was going to get from the house.'

23

Morrison allowed this first real admission to sink in. In the silence that followed, Neilson looked over the shoulders of his inquisitors far into the bare wall behind them. He wasn't thinking any longer what he should be saying or how to say it.

He wasn't thinking, he was just talking – in Panther speak. 'People believe all the lies about this Black Panther. The papers don't tell the truth about the Black Panther, so called. They tell lies about him. I read them, he not like how they say. I want tell you the truth, I hate all those lies. I want people to know the truth, I not tell you like the newspapers.'

Neilson had said more in these few inarticulate sentences than he'd said so far in all the interviews put together. 'Can you protect my wife and daughter if I make a statement?' he asked.

Morrison told him he couldn't make any promises, but he could arrange for him to see his wife as soon as possible as this was his right.

'I want to make a statement, I want everyone to know the truth. The girl need not have died if the money was paid.'

The officers then said that before they went ahead with any more questioning about Lesley Whittle, the murders they wanted to ask him about were those of Donald Skepper, Derek Anstin and Sydney Grayland. It took Neilson between five to ten minutes to reply after each name muttering, 'My God, this looks bad for me, but I want to tell the truth. It's not like the papers say.'

Neilson then started a marathon nine hours of statement relating to Lesley Whittle's kidnapping and death. This was followed by shorter statements relating to the murders at Harrogate, Accrington and Langley, and with the attempted murders of Peggy Grayland, Constable Mackenzie and Gerald Smith, and finally the blackmailing of Lesley's mother for the £50,000 ransom.

The statements were masterpieces of admission of the basic facts blended with pulling up short of any intent to kill anybody, told with sufficient detail to have a ring of truth. Guns would go off accidentally when it came to postmasters taking a launch at him in protecting their homes and businesses – and in the case of Lesley Whittle herself, well, she had fallen off the narrow metal platform in another accident as he came down the ladder and she moved over to give him some room.

Today there would have been a further murder to add to the charges in the case of Gerald Smith, the security guard at the Freightliner depot. He died from his wounds unexpectedly a year after the attack, after an operation on his stomach and the removal of a bullet from his hand. This was carried out on 19 March 1976 on the anniversary of his initial discharge from hospital, but five days later he collapsed, and then died a day after that. As his death occurred more than a year after the shooting it failed in English law, as it stood then before 1996, to be classed as murder.

Meanwhile, as promised, Irene Neilson was allowed to see her husband. However, it was unlikely to have been an intimate affair as later Donald's solicitor complained that he'd been unable to see his client in order to take instructions without him being handcuffed to a prison officer and therefore having their conversation overheard. Irene would have been granted nothing different and, faced with her husband in handcuffs, struggling to make conversation with a man with a black eye, puffy lips and cut face would have been difficult. Donald, in the presence of the prison officers, would have been careful not to incriminate himself any further than he had already.

The protection given to him in his various appearances for remand at court were as much to protect him as to stop him escaping. There was one attempt by a member of the public to assault him after a remand when Neilson was being escorted back to the prison van covered in a grey blanket. His assailant got to within a few feet of him before being seized by the police, but it turned out he only wanted to give him a thumping in return for what he'd done to Lesley Whittle.

The magistrates at the committal proceedings, where they look at the evidence and see if there is enough on the face of it to merit going to a full trial in the Crown Court, were faced with 245 witness statements and details of 848 exhibits. However, on this occasion no witnesses were called and the statements only were formally tendered to the court to allow the nine charges against Neilson to be sent up to Stafford Crown Court for trial.

Barristers had now been chosen to advise and represent both the prosecution and the defence. Philip Cox QC was appointed as leading counsel for the prosecution. Cox had a distinguished war record, contributing to the development and use of radar in detecting German submarines attacking Allied shipping across the Atlantic. After the war he trained as a barrister and became Recorder of Northampton.

The defence team was led by Gilbert Gray QC. His advocacy became so famous that one of his colleagues remarked that he made you feel that English was your second language. Gray felt from the start that his client was not going to get a fair trial in Staffordshire as he was already too infamous and that any jury was going to be biased against him. So he made an application to the court for a change in venue in a pretrial review at Birmingham Crown Court on 30 May 1976. He explained to the judge that the extensive police enquiries into the case meant that a large number of people in Staffordshire had been affected, if not directly then indirectly through someone they knew, or the extensive coverage of the case in local newspapers or the media and the hostility that had been whipped up. However, the judge was not impressed by the argument and felt the publicity was so nationwide that it probably didn't make much difference where the trial was held.

Gray then pointed out that thousands of people had made statements during the investigation and that it was now sixteen months since Lesley's disappearance, and so it was nearly inevitable that members of the jury would be involved, or their friends or relatives. At this point the judge conceded the point on the number of local residents involved and ordered the case not be heard at Stafford. Two days later Oxford was chosen as the venue, and he informed that the first trial would deal solely with the Lesley Whittle kidnap and murder.

But it wasn't just the number of statements that had been taken – 200,000 people had been interviewed to reach those statements. At Kidsgrove Police Station there were 2.5 million cards in the index system and 30,000 recorded telephone calls. Not once on those cards, in the telephone calls or in the statements did the name of Donald Neilson appear.

Even now in prison on remand with a trial looming, he had to keep fit: 200 press-ups in his cell on his fingertips and an hour's running around the exercise yard until he ran himself to a standstill. And all the while he was being watched. Not just by prison staff or his wife on her visits, or his solicitors in legal visits trying to put together a defence, but quietly by other prisoners, watching this maniac doing his laps of the exercise yard before breakfast, watching him take his meals, watching for a chance when they might show that whether or not you'd killed sub-postmasters and beaten up their wives, nothing in the criminal code allowed you to string up a 17-year-old girl and allow her to die in the dark. He might be the fittest man in the British prison system, but for the prisoners this was a dead man walking.

24

The trial for the kidnap and murder of Lesley Whittle and the attempted murders of Gerald Smith and PC Mackenzie finally opened on the morning of Monday, 14 July 1976 in Oxford Crown Court. It was a sweltering hot day, the beginning of the notorious 1976 drought in a badly aired and over-full courtroom, with seventy members of the press alone. The judge, Mr Justice Mars-Jones, decided to cut the afternoon session by an hour and ordered that members of the jury could take off their ties and jackets and counsel could remove their wigs in an attempt to stop everyone overheating.

The court was housed in the old county hall and was looking its age even in 1976. It was a wonderful example of early Victorian Gothic architecture without any of the advantages of the modern court, least of all air conditioning to replace the large round-topped windows that opened with cords the length of bell ropes to let in a gasp of fresh air that couldn't compete with the tropical conditions outside. Each morning the ushers would open the windows, tugging at catches that hadn't been oiled for decades like bell ringers at morning service, and then close them with less ceremony at the close of play.

The court was reached through the main hall, around which hung the remains of Oxford's eighteenth-century militia flags, where solicitors, clients and their barristers would meet first thing in a flurry of activity to discuss the day's tactics, often having to stand because there was nowhere to sit and grateful to have a cup of tea and biscuit provided on a stall run by the Women's Voluntary Service Corps, with the option of a chocolate Penguin if things were going well.

For Donald Neilson, charged with kidnapping, demanding with menaces and murder, being able to meet his legal team in the hall was not a luxury he could enjoy. He had been transferred from Birmingham's Winson Green Prison to a cell in Oxford Gaol, from where he was escorted underground through a 140-yard tunnel to emerge in the dock in the centre of the court. This is a dramatic moment at the beginning of the proceedings when the accused pops up into the dock like a jack-in-the-box, giving the chance for everyone in court to see whether the man looks like the ogre portrayed in the press and media or whether – just perhaps – it's all been a terrible mistake.

Certainly the man who emerged that morning looked anything but a kidnapper and murderer. He was dressed in a dark green suit with a tie, his hair was washed and fashionably curled down over his collar, and his face was fresh and almost youthful for a man of nearly 40. He was short, only 5ft 4in, wiry and athletic-looking, as if he kept himself in trim. But in contrast to most people in court who'd been sunbathing in the heatwave, Neilson looked pale after spending the last seven months in prison. Some put the way he looked down to his living in drain shafts, only coming out at night to pounce on young girls like Lesley Whittle and take them back to his lair.

Mr Justice Mars-Jones, like his prosecuting counsel, had served in the Royal Navy in the war and had earned a reputation as a fair but strict judge, a snob and a talented musician. His father had run the local post office in Wales – a fact that might have not endeared a man facing murder charges connected with raids on sub-post offices to him. Mars-Jones attended Aberystwyth University and, although obtaining a first in law, had not taken the usual Oxbridge route in becoming a High Court judge. He had prosecuted in the Moors Murder trial and as a judge would again encounter Gilbert Gray (Neilson's defence counsel) as defending counsel in the Nezar Hindawi case, when he passed on the defendant the longest ever prison sentence in this country – forty-five years.

Donald Neilson, as typical of him with his disregard for climate conditions, took no notice of the judge's concession to the heat and kept both his suit jacket and tie firmly on.

Before a jury could be sworn in, one important issue had to be sorted out so the trial could begin. This was the matter of whether the charges relating directly to Lesley Whittle's kidnapping should be heard at the same time as the attempted murders of Gerald Smith and PC Mackenzie. No jury, at least in the opinion of the defence, was going to remain unbiased on the question of kidnap if they had to decide whether Donald Neilson had also tried to shoot a security guard and a policeman. The defence maintained that Neilson, in shooting Gerald Smith, was reacting to a sudden challenge or threat posed by Smith, while the PC Mackenzie incident, coming ten months after the kidnapping, related to the burglaries Neilson was planning at the time.

The prosecution could hardly object to providing a fair trial, but made it clear to the judge that the reason they wanted the attempted murders to be kept in was because they wanted to show that Neilson's main motive for wanting to kill Gerald Smith and PC Mackenzie was getting them out of the way so that they couldn't give evidence against him at any future trial, and this was precisely his motive in murdering Lesley Whittle. She had been more dangerous to him alive than dead.

The judge agreed with the defence argument, saying that the police shooting arose from an entirely different enterprise from the kidnap and, while it was difficult to imagine a stronger case than the shooting of Gerald Smith, it was a spontaneous shooting in contrast to the careful planning of the kidnap. This proved a logistical problem for the prosecution because they then had to ask for an adjournment and go through the piles of statements, taking out any reference to the two shootings.

Settling these legal issues paved the way to allowing the trial proper to begin after lunch. Donald Neilson was again brought up into the dock and asked by the clerk of the court to stand while the charges were read out to him: 'Firstly, that on or about 14 January 1975, at Highley, stealing and unlawfully carrying away Lesley Whittle against her will.'

The clerk asked Nielson how he pleaded to that charge, to which he unexpectedly replied, 'Guilty.' It was a dramatic moment. Most of those in court that afternoon had fully expected him to make a fight of all the charges.

'Secondly, that on about 14 January 1975, with a view to gain, making an unwarranted demand of £50,000 to Dorothy Whittle with menaces, a threat to kill Lesley Whittle.'

Again he was asked how he pleaded to this charge, and again came the reply, 'Guilty.' A sense of anti-climax hit the court. The Black Panther was going to admit it all and they'd be going home that afternoon.

'Thirdly, that on a date unknown between 13 January and 7 March 1975, at Kidsgrove, he did murder Lesley Whittle.'

There was a momentary pause before the clerk asked the prisoner how he pleaded to this third charge. Without hurrying, and looking straight over to the jury, Neilson replied firmly and loudly, 'Not guilty.'

They'd got their trial.

The swearing in of the jury caused further delay because the defence objected to two of the four lady jurors. The two jurors in question were both middle-aged women who might well have had daughters of Lesley's age and have difficulty in giving Neilson a fair trial. Reasons for the objection don't have to be given, and once two other jurors were put up without any objection then matters could proceed. A third juror, a man this time, was also rejected because he couldn't read the oath properly – he said he'd lost his glasses, usually a euphemism for being unable to read.

Philip Cox QC opened for the prosecution with a stark and factual account of the particulars of the case. Behind him was a massive array of exhibits, so extensive that the judge had to ask twenty members of the press to vacate their seats to make room for it all. The collection included two shotguns, two rifles, a part-empty quarter bottle of brandy, clothes, blankets, a sleeping bag, Thermos flasks and food. The collection even featured a scale model of the drainage system at Bathpool Park, a vital visual aid to understanding the complex system of tunnels, some dry and some wet, ladders and manholes.

Cox said Lesley was studying for her A levels at Wulfrun College, Wolverhampton, and showed the jury photographs of the house in Highley where she lived with her mother. The facts didn't need much embroidering as they told the story of the kidnap and the attempts to hand over the ransom. However, now that Neilson had pleaded guilty to the kidnap and demanding with menaces, the point of attack in the prosecution case had shifted to the part of the story to which only the defendant and his prisoner were witness: the question of whether Lesley was pushed over the side of the metal platform or fell accidentally.

Neilson, he said, had chosen the Whittle family as his target three years earlier when he read in a newspaper that the family was embroiled in a court case over the late George Whittle's will. From the article he could see the family was well off, running a successful coach business. He then spent the next three years preparing the kidnap in order to obtain a large sum of money without being caught.

At the same time he bought a pair of binoculars in Manchester to reconnoitre the ground at Bathpool Park, coils of wire to tether Lesley in Walsall, and a car in Sutton Coldfield, on every occasion using a false name and making sure that every one of these purchases was such a distance apart that it would be difficult to trace them later if they were found. This is the reason that it took the police nine months to find Lesley's captor after her abduction.

Mr Cox showed the jury the coil of wire with the three bolts on a loop at one end where it had been secured to the ladder, and the noose at the other that had been placed around Lesley's neck with its three bolts that would have to be secured with a spanner. He said the ladder end of the wire showed more corrosion than the noose end, and the explanation for this was that the wire had already been secured to the ladder for some time before the other end was attached to Lesley. This suggested that preparations to receive her had been in place long before the kidnapping. 'You have a picture of this wire waiting for the victim, members of the jury,' he said.

Lesley had been given a sleeping bag, a bottle of brandy and a Thermos of soup – they knew this because the items were found later in the drainage system. All the time Lesley was in the shaft she was naked in the sleeping bag; although there were some clothes available she had not been given any to wear.

Mr Cox went through the meticulous way in which Neilson had planned the execution of the kidnapping and the laying of the ransom trail. 'From the prosecution's point of view this is important because it was the failure of these carefully laid plans that led the accused to take Lesley Whittle's life by pushing her off the platform,' he added.

The main motive in Neilson wanting to kill her would have been to prevent her recognising him in the future, and that in turn would depend on whether he always wore his hood. 'One of the central features of this case is what opportunity did the girl have to identify him? Was he hooded *all* the time he was in the drain? Or did he relax his precaution of attempting to keep his identity from the girl?' asked Cox.

Assuming that Neilson kept up his monosyllabic, squeaky voice with the West Indian accent to disguise his voice, this brought it down to one question: did he ever take off his hood in Lesley's presence?

Cox made the point that much of the first day in captivity must have been spent in making tapes of Lesley setting out his demands. The police had found one tape that Neilson had abandoned and found trampled into the ground, and it was still just about playable to the court. Then, when that demand was never met and fresh tapes had to be made altering the drop to Bathpool Park, did Neilson in all those hours of close proximity to Lesley really keep his hood on the whole time to prevent her seeing his face, or was it more likely he wouldn't bother, knowing that he would kill her in the end anyway?

Mr Cox suggested that this was the fate Neilson had in mind for Lesley from the start. Why else put the wire noose around her neck when he could have put it around her wrist or ankle? 'I submit that the evidence points strongly to the fact that he went down there in order to push Lesley off the landing before making his escape. I suggest he was extremely frustrated. There was Lesley Whittle still alive in the shaft who, for all he knew, might very well be able to give important information that could lead to his identification,' continued Cox.

He questioned why it had been necessary to be so cruel to Lesley in keeping her naked, with very little food and tethered by her neck. He also asked, was it likely that Lesley fell over the side by accident when she'd been held captive there for days and would be only too aware of the width of the platform and how far she had to manoeuvre without falling over the side?

25

In his statement to the police, Neilson described how the idea of a kidnap had come to him and how he went about preparing for the operation. The whole idea had been to demand enough of a ransom to put an end to his life of crime. He got the idea from a newspaper article in which he read about a court case involving a dispute with Lesley's father's will. 'From the newspaper I got the address and bought maps to enable me to find the address. From the amount of the will and income I estimated that £50,000 would be sufficient for me to finish with crime and would not be too great a loss as it left a considerable amount – as seen from the will and income from the existing business.

'After reading a full report of the will and circumstances I reckoned that the mother would immediately pay a ransom for this amount for the son, or alternatively the son for the mother. From maps I found the location of the house and business in summertime and also looked for a place where ransom could be collected.'

Neilson said he checked out Dudley Zoo as one collection point and then started looking for a second in a different area. 'I decided for a second collection point to be dropped from a train. I needed a railway line in a large open space with possibly a tunnel. From the map I followed the line and went by car to a parking space at the opposite end of Bathpool Park. I left the vehicle and walked the footpath along the railway. The footpath went past a concrete drain area and I came to an electricity substation. As I approached this I heard a roaring noise underfoot. I found the noise came from a slightly raised manhole cover. I raised the cover and saw a ladder going down into a shaft.

'I returned at a later date with a torch and went into the drainage system. After exploring the full complex I decided this could be used in some way for the collection. Next I found telephone boxes on a chosen route to be used for delivery of the ransom. Over a long period of time I visited all areas mentioned earlier to familiarise myself with the area.'

Neilson went on to describe, sometimes reverting to his idiosyncratic, abbreviated English, how he entered the house at Highley and took Lesley up to Bathpool Park, where he took her and some of the equipment down to the platform in the drainage shaft. 'I put the girl in another sleeping bag on top of the first. I gave her the survival blanket and bottle of brandy and tape recorder and flask of soup, and then sorted out the equipment and DYMO tapes. During the day I made all the DYMO tapes as required and girl taped the message on tape recorder by reading what I had written on writing pad in capitals.

'When dark I went out and took car to Walsall to commence putting out instructions for collection of ransom. All these were taped in telephone boxes. The last telephone box was outside the bus garage at Dudley. After completing laying instructions at Dudley Zoo I went back to telephone box at bus station with taped instructions on taped cassette that girl had made earlier that day with the ransom message to her mother. I dialled the three telephone boxes alternately at Swan Shopping Centre, Kidderminster, at approximately midnight. After a few times dialling all three dialling tones at other end went different, a kind of discontinued or engaged signal. Then I dialled for the last time and someone answering said, "Who is this?" I then rang off. As this voice was not normal and all

Lesley Whittle – the Black Panther's last victim.

'Beechcroft', Highley, the Whittle home from where Lesley was kidnapped.

Lesley's brother, Ronald, and mother, Dorothy. (*Murder Casebook*, Vol. 16)

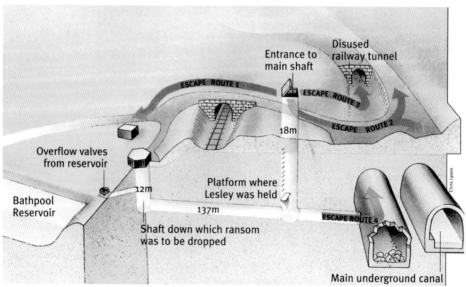

Disused railway tunnel

Entrance to main shaft

ESCAPE ROUTE 1

ESCAPE ROUTE 3

ESCAPE ROUTE 2

18m

Overflow valves from reservoir

Platform where Lesley was held

12m

Bathpool Reservoir

137m

Shaft down which ransom was to be dropped

ESCAPE ROUTE 4

Chris Lyons

Main underground canal

Bathpool Park drainage system. (*Murder in Mind*, Vol. 18)

The ledge in Bathpool Park on which Lesley was tethered. (Hawkes, *The Capture of the Black Panther*)

Above: The Glory Hole in Bathpool Park where the ransom was to be dropped. (Author's collection)

Right: Journalist posing in Black Panther's combat gear. (Hawkes, *The Capture of the Black Panther*)

Left: *Birmingham Evening Mail* front page, Wednesday 15 January 1975. (British Library)

Below: DCS Bob Booth with Neilson's abandoned car.

Right: The arresting officers outside 'The Junction' chippy, Rainworth. (Hawkes, *The Capture of Black Panther*)

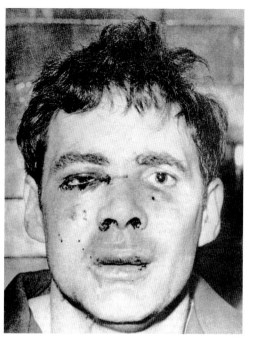

Above left: Donald Neilson after his arrest. (*Murder Casebook*, Vol. 16)

Above right: Shrouded under a blanket, Neilson on his way to court. (*Murder in Mind*, Vol. 18)

Right: The Neilsons' home in Bradford. (*Murder in Mind*, Vol. 18)

The Panther's lair in his Bradford home.

The Panther's combat kit.

Lesley Whittle's funeral.

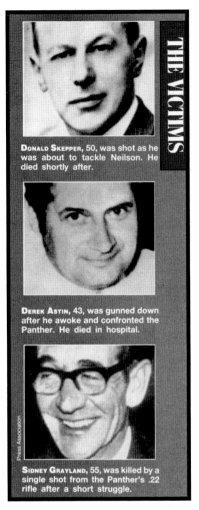

DONALD SKEPPER, 50, was shot as he was about to tackle Neilson. He died shortly after.

DEREK ASTIN, 43, was gunned down after he awoke and confronted the Panther. He died in hospital.

SIDNEY GRAYLAND, 55, was killed by a single shot from the Panther's .22 rifle after a short struggle.

Left: The three post office victims: Donald Skepper, Derek Astin and Sidney Grayland. (*Murder Casebook*, Vol. 16)

Below: Mr Gilbert Gray QC, Neilson's barrister. (*Murder in Mind*, Vol. 18)

Far left: Mr Justice Mars-Jones, the trial judge. (*Murder in Mind*, Vol. 18)

Left: Donald and Irene Neilson after their wedding in 1955.

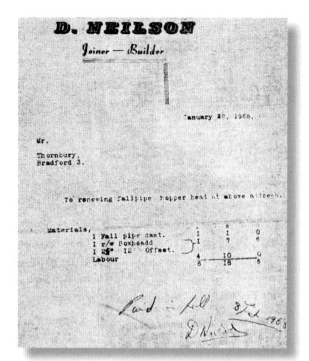

Invoice, D. Neilson, for repair work in 1968. (*Murder in Mind*, Vol. 18)

Daily Express, 17 May 1972 – the newspaper article that gave Neilson the kidnap idea.

three phone boxes were close together, I suspected a trap and returned to Bathpool. I returned to girl and made soup, using stove from car, and she had some. I explained there would be a delay. I left the car abandoned in the car park.

'I went back to girl and explained there would be a delay as tape recorder had broken and I could not send the message. During the period from then until the time I left to make the final telephone call we made new instruction tapes on the Philips tape recorder and new DYMO instructions. I left to make final telephone call arriving at telephone box at approximately midnight. I made the call and placed the tape into the phone. I thought at the time it was a male member of the Whittle family and a voice stated positively there would be no tricks. From the sincere tone of voice I fully believed the instructions would be carried out as I had been assured. I returned to the girl and told her they were bringing the money and it would take about two hours to get there and then she would be going home. I had presumed it was possible, if there was not any police, they would have put a bug in with the money. The depth of the drain underground would have made it not possible for them to follow the bug.

'I reckoned that with the many different entrances to all these tunnels and they not knowing location of the same this would give me ample time to return with the money to the girl, smash the bug and take out the girl with me to wait for them to find her. At no time did the girl see me. She could not possibly have recognised me by sight, description or from voice. There was positively no reason why the girl could not return to her family and give her family and the entire British Police Force every co-operation in trying to find me.

'So therefore there was positively no reason in doing the girl any harm. Even if the ransom was not paid there was positively no reason to do the girl any harm. If for any reason the ransom money was not collected that night there was no further collection point planned and the girl could not have been moved anywhere by me to give me time to look and plan a further collection point. If I did not wish to be caught the girl could have been left where she was or left at the top of the drainage system – whether or not the ransom had been paid – and I could have made my escape to safety.'

The final part of the statement deals with the final attempt at the collection of the ransom from Neilson's point of view and how he came to the conclusion that there was not only be going to be no drop but that a police operation had been set up to watch him. 'I went and removed the grill from the top of the shaft. From the top of the drainage cover I could see the point where the instructions said the car had to stop. I could also see if there had been anyone on foot. From memory I waited approximately one and a quarter hours. Then a car drove on to Bathpool from the direction of the instructions. This car stopped and turned lights out. From the time lapse it could have been a car sent by the police, if they had a phone tap out on the Whittle phone, or it could have been a courting couple whom I had seen other nights coming to Bathpool as late as 4.15 a.m.

'I waited and a few minutes later a car came into Bathpool and drove in the direction of the instructions I had phoned. It did not, however, carry out instructions I had passed over telephone. It then reversed quickly and went past the first car that had pulled in a drive along a dead-end track which runs parallel to the railway. From my position I fully believed I had no cause for alarm. My safety was not threatened in any way. I waited and began to doubt the sincerity of the man who answered the phone call. Approximately forty-five minutes later a helicopter passed overhead almost directly over me. It came round in half a circle and hovered some miles to the south of me. It seemed from this it was obvious this was a police trap in operation. I was not panicked.

'In the next few minutes the car that had driven along the dead-end track returned and went out of Bathpool. At this point I realised the money was not going to be paid. Minutes later the first car that entered Bathpool Park followed the dead-end track car out of Bathpool. I decided there was no point in waiting further.

'I entered the shaft through the grill opening and went along the tunnel after climbing into the short pipe leading to the platform. I saw the light from the other side as the girl had on her torch. As I came down from the short tunnel on to the platform she went over the side and was suspended by the wire I had placed there earlier to prevent her leaving the tunnel. I moved to the side of the platform that she had gone over. Her head was below the level of the platform. I saw her face. Her eyes seemed to be half closed and stopped moving. I froze, then panicked. The next thing I remember is shoving the cover up to get out. I then closed the cover.

'I stopped there for some moments unable to think what to do. I started to dash down from the top of the mound towards the disused railway line. I fell and a bag I had in my hand spilled its contents. I lay still for some moments, and then along a track that runs along the bottom of the ski slope I saw lights of a vehicle slowly moving towards this end of Bathpool. A car drove out of Bathpool towards Kidsgrove. I think the same car came back seconds later with no lights on.

'At this point I thought I was near to being surrounded. I started to collect the things and put them back in the bag. I heard the sound of dogs coming from, as far as I could tell, the dead-end track. I panicked and fled in the opposite direction.'

Mr Cox finished reading the statement and pointed out that Neilson had mentioned being hooded at the time of the kidnap, 'almost as an afterthought' only later in the statement. 'Above all he mentions the wire, you may think, as an afterthought. He mentions the wire that he had placed there to prevent her leaving. He mentions that he took the wire into the tunnel but he did not mention that he used it to restrain her until later in the statement.'

Mr Gilbert Gray, who as defence counsel had had little to do so far but listen to the prosecution case, now stood to read two formal admissions on behalf of his client, namely that on 14 January 1975 he kidnapped Lesley Whittle and took her to the third platform landing of the shaft of the Bathpool drainage complex at Kidsgrove, Staffordshire. Also that it was his intention to hold her for ransom and in pursuance of this made a demand for £50,000.

Neilson's statement that Lesley falling over the side of the platform was an accident rather than him pushing her over has a ring of truth about it. Had the wire not snagged on the stanchion there would have been enough slack for her to get her feet on to the bottom of the shaft – in other words, there was no guarantee that Lesley would have died by intentionally pushing her over the side anyway. It was Neilson's belief that the police had him surrounded and so would have found her sooner rather than later. The only way he could have guaranteed her death would have been to shoot her, like he did all his other victims.

The statement describes his paranoia about a police trap, as he starts hearing helicopters and dogs closing in as part of the police operation. Without a minute to waste, he starts running down the hill from the glory hole, falling over and dropping his holdall as he does, pausing only to scoop some of the more important contents back into the bag, but ditching the sugar buns and Thermos flask of soup. He's on foot and has his gun and pistol and can deal with anyone trying to arrest him. He has no getaway vehicle and if he can get out of the park on foot he can catch a train and look like any other early morning worker.

It worked. The most important thing about this, and any other operation, as he repeatedly told the police and the court, was to get away a free man. The money would have been nice, but he was free to live another day. The fate of his victim, like all the others, was less important.

26

Ronald Whittle, Lesley's elder brother, was now called as a prosecution witness. At 32, he looked surprisingly young to be the managing director of the family firm, serious and drawn, now having to come face to face with the man accused of murdering his young sister. He wore a smart double-breasted suit and a colourful tie, clutching the rails of the witness box in grim determination as he gave his evidence.

More demands had been made on him than any other member of the Whittle family during the case. He'd been one of the first to see the DYMO tape saying that Lesley had been kidnapped. He'd then been responsible for informing and working with the police, trying to comfort his mother and keeping the lid on the family business as the investigation progressed. Not least was trying to work out where the various drops of the ransom were meant to be taking place by deciphering obscure instructions, trying to find the messages themselves hidden in telephone boxes, and at the same time dealing with a number of cruel and time-wasting hoaxes from members of the public until it reached the point of only dealing with demands if there was some concrete proof that they were genuine.

Even when it came to the real thing, when they knew the instructions were coming from the kidnapper himself, his frustration can only be imagined at missing the first telephone call on the first evening of the kidnap, followed by no call on the second, and then the desperate search to follow the instructions on the third. How many times must he have wished he'd never contacted the police who, with the best will in the world, were continually slowing the process?

Ronald now explained to the court that on the evening of 16 January at 11.45 p.m. a call had been taken by his manager with Lesley's recorded voice telling him to go to a telephone box in Kidsgrove outside the post office, where there would be a further message telling him where to go next. When he reached the telephone box he had a lot of difficulty finding the message behind the backboard in the telephone box and it was only at the third attempt that he found it at all.

The tape read:

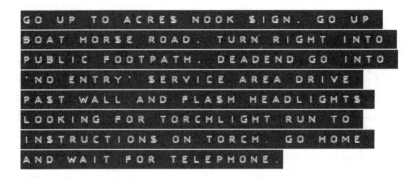

GO UP TO ACRES NOOK SIGN. GO UP BOAT HORSE ROAD. TURN RIGHT INTO PUBLIC FOOTPATH. DEADEND GO INTO 'NO ENTRY' SERVICE AREA DRIVE PAST WALL AND FLASH HEADLIGHTS LOOKING FOR TORCHLIGHT RUN TO INSTRUCTIONS ON TORCH. GO HOME AND WAIT FOR TELEPHONE.

He then went back to the car and wrote out the instructions to make sure he'd got them right. Next he drove up Boat Horse Lane and turned right into the car park. There was no one in the car park and there was no sign of a wall, so he continued past the 'No Entry' signs and along the road until he came to a bridge going over the road and a dam beyond that. This was the first sign of any walls and so he flashed his lights. There was no sign of any response and so he drove further on down the road looking for walls, until he came to part of the road with low walls either side. Again he flashed his headlights and again without any response. He then drove even further along the road and under a railway bridge and another car park, and flashed his lights again. When he received no response he drove back to the first bridge and the dam, flashing his lights the whole time. He then turned round and repeated the whole process. This all took at least half an hour and he then drove home, arriving at 5.30 a.m. and giving the message tape to Mr Booth.

Mr Gray stood up to cross-examine. 'I don't want to pry into general methods of detection,' he said, doing just that, 'but did you understand that methods of electronic bugging devices were being used?'

'I can't recall whether it was that night or one of the many other calls,' Ronald replied. 'You see, there were a number of hoax calls during this time and we used the same procedure on each occasion.'

'Yes, I understand,' said Mr Gray. 'Did the police tell you that they would be nearby if you needed help?'

'Yes, the police told me they would be in the vicinity with a control van as I went to make the money drop. I was fitted with radios, both on me and on my car and I was told to keep the police informed of developments.'

'You were given to understand the police would be ready, willing and able to back you up rather smartly if anything occurred?'

'I was told that there would be a delay but that they would be with me if anything happened, yes.'

Finally Ronald explained how his sister was regarded by relatives and friends alike as a happy, sensible and easy-going teenager and a very nice person to get on with.

The pathologist Dr John Brown told the court that death was almost instantaneous resulting from vagal inhibition due to compression by hanging by the neck from a wire rope around the neck. The platform was encrusted with rust and any attempt to haul the body back up would have resulted in abrasions to the body and there were no such signs on the body. Nor was there any sign of resuscitation, and in any event for there to be resuscitation the collar would have had to be removed from the neck.

The autopsy showed the body of a well-nourished young female with a height of 5ft 2¾in, weighing 98lb. The body gave the appearance of being somewhat dehydrated, without any recent meal in the three days before her death.

He explained to the court that although Lesley died almost instantaneously, in that her heart stopped beating, her brain would have gone on living for several more minutes and had attempts to revive been done quickly there was a chance she would have recovered. There were no signs on her body that Neilson had tried to revive her, nor that he had attempted to drag her back up on to the platform. It was suggested that Lesley had been in her sleeping bag as she went over the side of the platform. A yellow sleeping bag was found in the canal system when drained. Mr Cox suggested that if she'd been wrapped in the sleeping bag when she struggled with Neilson as he pushed her over the side then there might be no marking of her body. Dr Brown said that apart from the neck there was singularly little evidence of violence on Lesley's body. Had a determined effort been made at external cardiac massaging after the hanging, it might well have succeeded.

Mr Gray cross-examined. 'But, Dr Brown, you're not seriously suggesting that in these circumstances the accused would have had the wherewithal to administer this sort of first aid?'

'Well, I agree a layman would have thought all that too late because there would at that stage be no pulse or breathing.'

When it was Sergeant Perriton's turn to give evidence, one of the police officers who'd actually found Lesley's body in the shaft on 7 March eight weeks after the kidnap, Mr Gray put a question that had occurred to many in the courtroom. 'Despite Lesley mentioning in the taped message to her mother on 16 January last year that she'd got a bit wet, no one had put two and two together and thought of searching the underground drainage system at Bathpool Park at that stage. Didn't anyone know of the wet conditions in Bathpool Park?'

'Not until I got there, I don't believe they did,' replied Perriton. 'You couldn't put two and two together until I got there. Until I had been down the shaft, no.'

'Do you know why it was,' persisted Gray, 'that Bathpool Park, which had a drainage complex, was not searched in January?'

'No sir, I do not.'

'Were Scotland Yard involved in the search at this stage?'

'Yes sir, they were involved from the start. But it was Detective Chief Superintendent Booth who ordered me to search the system – not a Yard man.'

The next two police officers gave evidence about the state they found Neilson in immediately after his arrest. Detective Sergeant Andrew Ford of Mansfield Police said that Neilson had been sitting in a CID office wrapped in a blanket when he had first seen him at 12.45 a.m. on 16 December 1975.

Mr Gray said there was no question that the police were responsible for the beating Neilson received after his arrest. 'I don't want to go into the reasons for it, but he wasn't in a very good physical condition, was he?'

'He'd obviously been beaten around the head,' replied Ford. 'His right eye was cut, he had one or two cuts to his right cheek and both his eyes were beginning to puff up. Both of his nostrils had been bleeding and there was congealed blood around them. His lips were also beginning to puff up and were bruised.' Ford added that Neilson had been very tense when approached, and photographs taken of him next morning showed that he'd been cleaned up a little. The acting police surgeon had been called in to stitch his wounds.

Detective Chief Superintendent Readwin, as head of Nottingham CID, said he'd found it difficult to establish a rapport with Neilson and for the first one-and-a-half hours his answers to questions had been monosyllabic. He had at first refused to give even his name and address to protect his family, but they shook hands on a deal where Neilson would be co-operative if he could have contact with his wife. The handshake had been unusual, but Readwin hadn't wanted to destroy the rapport he'd managed to build over two hours.

The last of the police officers to give evidence was the man who'd led the police investigation, Detective Chief Superintendent Bob Booth himself, looking every inch the policeman with a portly countenance, a tie fastened with a clip over a generous middle-aged spread, bristle moustache and a look that said he didn't suffer fools. He was a man who felt wronged, not only by an investigation that had gone wrong resulting in the death of a young girl and a terrible ordeal while they'd tried to find her, but a resentment of colleagues from different police forces that led to confusion and animosity, bordering on farce and running hand in hand with plain bad luck.

The culmination of the farce was when an illuminated police car from Staffordshire Police Force arrived at the Bathpool Park car in the early hours of 17 January just as the attempted drop was about to take place by Ronald Whittle. The police car, apparently unaware that a stake-out was in progress, swept in to take the numbers of any unidentified vehicles, including that of a courting couple trying to get a little privacy, and members of West Mercia Police positioned throughout a 6-mile radius ready to come to Ronald's help should he need it.

Mr Booth couldn't contain himself and was going to use this opportunity to vent his spleen on the internal conflict going on between his troops, whether or not it was relevant to the trial. He told the court that Scotland Yard had offered technical and manpower assistance to West Mercia Police a few hours after news of the kidnap, and he had accepted. The £50,000 in notes that Ronald was to take to Kidsgrove were each micro-filmed and he was fitted with a personal transmitter. The suitcase itself was not bugged, but police cars had travelled at a discreet distance ahead and behind Ronald as he made his way to Bathpool Park.

Like Ronald, the police party had got a little lost on the way, but had managed to find the area and set up surveillance. Staffordshire Police had been informed and twelve Scotland Yard cars were in position helping with surveillance. Booth himself was positioned in a control centre in the appropriately named Mow Cop, 6 miles from the drop zone. He repeated that the local force had been told to keep away.

Mr Gray asked him if he'd thought about the operation in the months since then.

'To the point of distress that it should be revealed in court this morning to these people and the public at large to know,' he replied. He added that, on the morning after the failed drop, Scotland Yard had returned to the park to make a search of the area. He was not happy with the situation.

'Did they find anything?' asked Gray.

'Not a scrap,' Booth replied.

'Were you appalled when later so many items of evidence were found in Bathpool Park?'

'The police forces came out of this in a poor light. Yes, of course I was disgusted.'

At the conclusion of the prosecution case Mr Gray must have been tempted to submit that there was insufficient evidence to proceed with the case on the question of Lesley's death. The only witness to her death was Neilson himself. The rest of the evidence was vague, and while it is likely the case would have proceeded, there was always the danger that when a defendant like Donald Neilson was put in the witness box he would dig a deeper hole for himself.

27

onald Neilson looked anything but a black panther as he made his way over the courtroom to the witness box. There was none of the marching stride with the swinging arms, no confidence or swagger; his shoulders were stooped in a pose that would have been screamed at by a sergeant major on parade. He stood nervously in the box, the wild animal in him now tamed, his jaw working and his eyes looking furtively over to the barristers and then up to the judge, wondering who was going to ask him the first question.

But in Donald Neilson's eyes he had long promoted himself from squaddie to officer rank, the man responsible not just for the execution of the operation, but for its planning and logistical preparation as well. He spoke in a soft Yorkshire accent, as he got into his stride, his shoulders and chin coming back up, his hands joined in front of him.

Before deciding on the drainage shaft at Bathpool Park as the hiding place for his victim, he said, he had considered a number of other possibilities. 'This was the most difficult part of the plan for it had to be done by one man. There was nobody who could stay with the prisoner the entire time and therefore what I needed was somewhere that was soundproofed where the prisoner did not have to be gagged.

'I needed somewhere where they could move around and didn't need to be bound. I needed somewhere where there could be light that didn't show out when I wasn't there. I thought of one or two ideas. I considered renting one or two garages and in one making a soundproofed room. One way would have been to put in a garden shed.' But he had made and sold garden sheds for a living and so this was ruled out because of the possibility of his being connected with the crime. 'I then thought of soundproofing a garage by building a separate room inside it. This would have been all right for sound but I am not very good at figures and I have no way of working out exactly the amount of air that would be inside the soundproofed room. So I had to abandon that idea. Another possibility would be a boat. If it was a boat it could have been left in a disused canal tunnel and this would give freedom to the prisoner who could be free to move but not escape. The difficulty with that scheme would be finding a boat that I wouldn't be connected with. If I bought one it was possible it might be remembered.'

Neilson explained how he had discovered the Bathpool drainage system while looking at the railway line and planning that money would be dropped from a train on to the line. When he was on the footpath and heard a sound below the ground, made by water coming from a pipe, he lifted the drain cover and saw that it went further down. 'Eventually I realised that the ideal place to cover every eventuality would be at the bottom of the main shaft at Bathpool Park.' He had chosen to tether his victim at the neck with a wire leash because he'd expected it to be Lesley's brother, Ronald. If the leash had been attached to the wrist, ankle or waist it would have been easier for a victim, particularly a man, to have broken it by rubbing it against ironwork or concrete in the shaft. It might also have been possible to slip it off a limb made soft and slippery by water.

Neilson said that he went to the house in Highley expecting to kidnap Ronald Whittle. He said he had never threatened Lesley with a gun and that there was no sexual motivation in the case.

Mr Gray then asked Nelson if he had a daughter of his own. At this point Neilson's voice cracked and he sobbed briefly. In the end he just nodded.

The subject then turned to the sort of voice he was using at the kidnap and while he held Lesley hostage in the shaft to avoid recognition afterwards. Neilson described the voice he used as 'harsh, a voice of command', and he then gave a demonstration to the court. The tone went up an octave and came across in a staccato West Indian accent or, as one journalist in court described it, a squawk. 'You have been kidnapped. Stay still and you okay. If not behave you go in boot. Okay?'

Neilson said that when he said this in the car going to Bathpool Park, Lesley simply groaned – not that she had much option as she was gagged and lying under two foam mattresses at night in the back of a stranger's car. One can imagine, if it is possible to imagine, her being ushered down wet, dark tunnels being squawked at by some man in a hood with a gun and chained by the neck with a wire, as a descent into hell, with the best hope that this was some sort of nightmare from which she hadn't awoken in the night.

Gray asked Neilson, 'Did you kill Lesley Whittle?'

'No sir,' he replied firmly.

'Did you ever intend or expect harm to come to Lesley Whittle?'

'No sir,' was the clear reply again.

Neilson explained that he'd got the idea of a kidnap from reading a report in the *Daily Express* four years ago of a court case involving the Whittle family and a disputed will of £300,000. He'd learnt there were two children, Ronald and Lesley, and he thought £50,000 was a reasonable sum to ask of them as they wouldn't miss it that much.

He reconnoitred Highley and Bathpool Park and thought the latter a good spot to keep a prisoner as any bug placed with a ransom wouldn't operate so far underground. He said the night he picked for the kidnap would depend entirely on weather conditions, and on the night itself he parked the car in the village car park at Highley at about 2 a.m. and came through a council estate on a footpath leading behind the house. Once inside the house he checked the kitchen for a dog bowl or dog food. Then he went back out to fetch the car and left it in the lane facing downhill beside the house. He cut the telephone wire and was carrying a torch and shotgun.

Counsel asked him, 'Were you intending to use that shotgun?'

'No,' Neilson replied. 'From the time I went into the garage I had a hood on. I had it open, on the top of my head until I went upstairs. I then went up the stairs with the hood on, and crossed the landing, with one board creaking. Across the landing I could see one bedroom door open. I could see slightly by the light of the streetlamps outside.'

At this point in court there was a thump on the floor and a kerfuffle from the public gallery. A woman had fainted and the judge halted proceedings for a moment while the ushers went to help and escorted her out of the hot and crowded courtroom. The doors were opened and kept open to try to circulate some air.

After a sip of water and some more throat clearing, Neilson went on to explain that at this stage he couldn't tell whether the person in bed was a man or a woman, even when he shone the torch in the person's face after they had woken up.

'When did you realise it was a girl?' Gray asked.

'When she got out of bed. At that time I thought it was a young woman.'

'What made you think that?'

'She had nothing on,' replied Neilson.

There was a deadly hush in the court, accentuated by the heat and lack of air, interrupted only by counsel asking the accused to carry on with his account. 'I said something like, "Money, where's the money?" I wanted to sound gentle, positive,' said Neilson, speaking quietly now in an undertone, as if he was back in that bedroom.

Everyone was looking over to him, anxious not to miss a word, but already wondering how waking a young girl in the night, shining a torch in her face and having her step naked out of bed at the end of a gun with a man wearing a black hood was ever going to sound gentle and positive.

'Was it your ordinary voice, or not?' asked Gray.

'It was an assumed voice. I used sentences of two or three words. At that time it was essential there was no alarm. For this reason the manner of the voice, or manner, had to be in no way hostile. In answer to my question she said it was in the bathroom, £200 to £300 in change or in coin.'

'Did you know where the bathroom was?'

'I asked her to show me. She dressed and then we walked along the landing. A board creaked and I thought I heard a noise from another bedroom. She stopped and from her manner and the look on her face she looked as though she didn't want to wake anybody. I motioned her to go downstairs and we left the house the way I'd come in through the garage. I asked her again about the money. And then I left her in the garden and went back into the house and left the DYMO tape on the vase in the front room. When I came back she was still standing there in the same position. I said to her, "Are you cold?" and she nodded. I said, "You come in car while I get money."'

Neilson said he then put tape around her eyes, telling her this was so she wouldn't see the car. He had already taped her hands and mouth. He carried Lesley to the car and she climbed into the back seat. He covered her with two foam mattresses about 6ft 2in long so that no one could see her from outside.

After he drove off towards Kidsgrove and after driving for some distance, he heard a sound from the back seat. He stopped the car and put the mask back over his face in case Lesley removed the tape from her eyes. He spoke to her in his pidgin English and when she accepted what he said he talked to her in a friendlier tone, although still using the pidgin English. He asked her if she was warm enough, put the tape back on her mouth and as they resumed their journey to Bathpool Park he made sure the car heater was full on.

Once down the shaft and settled on the metal platform, he said he gave Lesley biscuits, puzzles, taped music and some coloured napkins that he thought would be pleasant for her. She reacted well to all this, he claimed, and seemed bright-eyed and not all depressed or upset through her ordeal. He gave her a bottle of brandy and she clutched it and said, 'For me? Super!' 'The whole purpose was that there should be no hostility between us. I needed her to make the ransom tapes. It was essential that these tapes were made in her voice and with her phrasing and that they showed no sign of tension.'

As he gave his evidence, Neilson would sometimes pause to sip a glass of water, his eyes welling up and looking as if he might burst into tears.

He wanted to be painted as the kidnapper who worried about his victim's well-being, making things as comfortable as possible, equally portraying the victim as near content as a victim could be, not resisting and grateful for her little luxuries such as the brandy, the tapes of selected pop music and coloured napkins that she might even use to decorate the platform and make it home.

'If at any time I'd noticed that she was sickening or that her eyes had gone dull or glazed, I would have taken her out of the drainage shaft that was her cell,' he explained. But inevitably the mask slipped as he went on with his evidence. He relived what went on down in the shaft one evening when he registered his surprise as he returned to find Lesley sheltering from falling mud and dirt under a plastic sheet.

'How did you register your surprise?' asked Mr Gray.

'There must have been something in my face – my expression,' Neilson replied.

'But did you not have your hood on at the time?'

'Then it must have been my manner,' said Neilson, probably by now realising his slip. Certainly the jury had, because they were whispering among themselves.

He told the jury that on the days he had held Lesley in the shaft he had gone back home to Bradford in the afternoon to have a sleep and to make a show of being around in case the neighbours had noticed he was missing. He made the journey of 120 miles driving his stolen Morris 1100 to Halifax and then taking the forty-minute bus ride to Bradford.

It was from the first of these journeys that he brought back what he called the 'comforts', including two plastic puzzles from the attic of his home, the coloured napkins, a tin of assorted biscuits and some magazines to keep her occupied. Also on the journey he had called into shops in the Oldham area and bought her some paperback books, a newspaper, chewing gum, mints and some chicken legs from a fish and chip shop. Later on in the journey he stopped his car in a lay-by and recorded some light music from the radio on to a cassette that he intended to leave with Lesley.

Neilson explained how he transported Lesley from home to Bathpool Park wearing only a candlewick dressing gown and bedroom slippers. Gagged, blindfolded and with hands bound she'd been led through subterranean tunnels, walking in swift-flowing water sometimes 5–6in deep. He had tried to carry her like a child but had been unable to do so because the roof of the tunnel was too low. 'I kept reassuring her it was okay,' he said, 'and that she could get dry soon. When we reached the platform I told her to take off her dressing gown to get it dried.'

'Did she appear to be frightened or apprehensive at being unclothed in such close proximity to you?' Mr Gray asked.

'She didn't show anything in that way,' Neilson replied.

'What were you about when she was drying herself? Were you looking or turning away?'

'My thoughts at that time were only to get out and move my car. It was getting light. She had her back to me. She then got into her sleeping bag and I never saw her out of it after that. My main fear was of the victim suffering hypothermia or pneumonia due to the sudden change in temperature.'

'Did she ever complain about anything you were doing to her?' asked counsel.

'Never, not even when I put the wire around her neck.'

'Why had you decided to use a five-foot length of wire rope to secure her?'

'I used that to give her the freedom. She could go anywhere she liked within the length of the wire. She was in the sleeping bag when I attached the wire but showed no signs of fear. I used bulldog clips to fasten the wire around her neck, tightening at least two of them with a spanner. I wrapped plaster around the tether to stop it coming into contact with her skin and chafing it.'

Counsel paused a moment to take a sip of water. The difficulty with this sort of questioning was that while his client might have shown a morsel of consideration for Lesley in giving her some movement space and by plastering the noose to give her a little more comfort, the bigger question was why was he putting her through this ordeal in the first place?

'Did she co-operate in making the tape recordings with instructions to the family?' counsel continued.

'Yes, she co-operated fully with all that. To enable her to do this I carried with me, taped to my stomach and wrapped in polythene, a prompting card with the words "Send personal message. Tell them you okay." This was followed by the ransom trail instructions. On the last day when I told her I'd triggered the ransom trail and that her brother was on the way with the money, she looked very happy. I explained I had to be up at the top to be there when he arrived so that there would be no misunderstanding. She wanted to come with me.'

'You say she wanted to come with you, but what arrangements had you made for her release?'

'I'd prepared for her release by bringing trousers, socks, a jumper and a pair of brown running shoes for Lesley to wear on her release.'

'Was this clothing bought especially for her?'

'No, this was all clothing I'd originally bought for myself. When I showed it to her she brightened up a lot. I recall that when I showed her the size seven shoes, she said, "These for me? They're huge."'

Remembering this little incident with Lesley down in the shaft, the sort of scene he might have had with his own daughter at home sorting out some walking shoes, Neilson paused again and was trying to stop himself bursting into tears.

28

As the heatwave in the country continued, conditions became unbearable in court by the early afternoon, and the judge decided that the best way through this was to get as much as possible of the day's hearing done in the morning and allow the court to rise in the early afternoon. Another lady had fainted, and the court looked on as she had been taken out of the courtroom to revive. But the atmosphere in court became one of survival as Neilson, now in his third day in the witness box, compared his conduct of the kidnap to a military operation.

He said he'd gained experience serving with the King's Own Yorkshire Light Infantry and had regarded the police as the enemy. He had assessed their possible tactics by studying other cases. If he had been the police, he said, he would have used two SAS marksmen with night-sights to pick off a criminal like himself.

Neilson's performance in the witness box became noticeably more enthusiastic when he started talking about his master plan for the crime, and decidedly shirty if the judge or counsel had the temerity to suggest the plan was faulty. It wasn't the plan that was faulty, it was the implementation of the plan.

So when it came to Lesley's death, this was not in the plan, and was the greatest unforeseen mishap of the whole operation. It was on the night of 16 January after the failed drop at Bathpool Park. The court had already heard what Neilson had to say about this in his statement to the police, as it had been read out by Mr Cox, but now they had a chance to hear what he said live in the witness box and then face cross-examination from the prosecution.

Neilson began by telling the court that by that stage in the night, with traffic coming in and out of the park but still no one carrying out his instructions by flashing their lights and coming across with the money, he was convinced that the police were setting a trap. So he went down the shaft for the last time in order to free Lesley and then make his escape.

'As I descended I saw Lesley had started to move as she normally did to allow me to get off the ladder on to the platform beside her. She moved away from the ladder and to her right as she was lying. As I stepped from the ladder I had one foot on the landing. I took my foot off the ladder and turned and it was while I was doing this that I looked round and she went over. The lantern was still lit. I grabbed this and stepped across to the other side of the landing. I put one foot down on the concrete ledge and went down into a squatting position in front of her. I had the lantern in my right hand and I held my left hand down towards her with the intention of pulling her back up. But her head was lower than the gantry and she was hanging with one shoulder underneath it.'

No one moved in court. Even the public gallery, occupied mostly by women since an hour before the court started that morning, sat motionless. Lesley's mother, Dorothy Whittle, sat there inert, inscrutable behind her large glasses.

'There was some movement and her right hand was stretched out behind her, moving. Her other arm bent at the elbow with the fist clenched. There was nothing for me to grab hold of. The torch was pointing into her face. Her eyes flickered and stopped. There was no movement. It was then I realised she was dead.'

Neilson stopped there for a moment to regain his composure. He was staring at the floor in front of him and beads of perspiration were standing out on his forehead. 'This stopped me dead in my tracks. She was dead,' he repeated. 'There was absolutely nothing I could do and I am telling this court that from the time I stepped on to the landing until the time of her being dead would be somewhere in the region of three to four seconds.'

Neilson said he didn't agree with what the pathologist Dr Brown had said about Lesley's heart stopping beating but her brain going on living for several minutes, and that resuscitation would have been possible. 'I don't accept that evidence. It wasn't my choice to be there but I saw her die. It wasn't my choice to see it. But I still say she died in four seconds although I didn't time it.'

'Did you push her off the platform?' asked Mr Gray.

'I did not, sir,' came the emphatic reply.

Mr Gray went on to ask if Neilson felt he'd formed any sort of relationship with Lesley. 'I did not try to form a relationship with the girl. There was no relationship at all, but it is my belief that there was an understanding between us. It was essential for my plan that my conduct be proper and correct at all times and hers certainly was.'

He said that he had the third, less risky, alternative of leaving her tied down in the shaft in the knowledge that the police would discover her from clues he had left on the surface. He had not wanted to kill Lesley because throughout the operation she had been his ace and would continue to be of importance afterwards. The information that she would give to the police when she came out would not have allowed them to pursue the same campaign of hatred. They would have been in a position of having a kidnap victim who had been well treated. He had planned the operation in army style, preparing himself to a level of super-physical fitness with long cross-country treks, running and walking.

In the closing stages of his evidence, Neilson tried to explain why he might have made any incriminating remarks about himself to the police, including referring to himself as the Black Panther. 'I didn't know where I was or where I was going,' he said. 'My arrest came eleven months after Lesley's kidnap and death, and this had come as a major psychological shock for me. In a very short period of time everything had come to an end. In the months since the kidnap I had erased the whole episode from my mind. Having it suddenly brought back through police questioning has confused and upset me enough to make me say things I didn't mean.'

'The prosecution are suggesting that you put these things out of your mind because you have a 16-year-old daughter and you are unable to live with what you did to Lesley,' said Mr Gray.

This time Neilson merely shook his head violently. 'There was just no need for me to remember it. The whole thing was closed from my mind from the night it happened.'

When it now came to the turn of Mr Philip Cox to cross-examine, the gloves were off. 'Mr Neilson, the truth was that after snatching Lesley Whittle from her home in the early hours of that morning, you terrorised her and transported her trussed on the floor of your stolen car,' Mr Cox began.

'I did not terrorise her, sir,' replied Neilson.

'You were carrying a sawn-off shotgun and wearing a cartridge belt, isn't that true?'

'Yes, but I never intended to use them and had conditioned myself to abandon the kidnap if resistance had been shown.'

'You were wearing a black hood with two eyeholes. Wouldn't that be enough to instil fear into your victim?'

'Yes, but this was more to avoid being recognised rather than to frighten the victim.'

'Perhaps you could show us then by putting on one the hoods we have of yours,' said Mr Cox, looking away from the accused as if he expected an objection to this suggestion from the defence.

Sure enough Mr Gray got to his feet. 'Before he does that, my Lord, I should warn my client that his wearing a hood in the witness box is likely to create a visual impact likely to disturb or alarm the jury.'

Neilson then turned to the judge. 'In the circumstances, my Lord, I would prefer not to.'

'Very well, but I suppose you realise, Mr Neilson,' continued Cox, 'that you frightened this girl out of her wits?'

'She was not, sir. Not at any time.'

'You don't consider that being blindfolded, gagged and having her hands taped behind her back was going to terrify her?'

'No sir, she co-operated by never trying to run away or attract attention. I found no need to truss her and would have hesitated to do so.'

'And are you seriously telling us that you had no idea that it was Lesley you were going to abduct rather than her brother or mother? How many times had you visited Highley and reconnoitred the area around her home while you were hatching your plot?'

'I am saying that. I visited the area at least ten times in the three years I was planning the operation and I still didn't know whether it would be Lesley, her brother or her mother who would be the victim. When I did discover it was Lesley in the bedroom and that she was unclothed I went through with the plan and never took advantage of her. I treated her nakedness as a matter of fact. My feelings throughout the time were ones of detachment in the same way that a doctor accepts a patient in hospital. He has professional detachment.'

Neilson seemed to be listening to himself describing himself as the professional, pulling himself up to his full 5ft 4in and clutching the front of the witness box like a captain on his bridge, doing the job oblivious to the human frailties that lesser men might be party to.

'You surely don't say you just regarded this business as a military operation, pitting your wits against the police?' asked Mr Cox.

'The operation itself came first,' replied Neilson adamantly, looking over to the jury. 'The most important point in any crime is to be free at the end of it. The money, the ransom, was not the most important issue. Freedom at the end of the plan was the most important issue.'

'So when you said in your message on the punched tape to the Whittle family, "Police or tricks – death", you are telling us you didn't really mean it?'

'That's right – it wasn't to be taken literally. It's the same if I fit a silencer to a gun,' Neilson replied, tapping his finger on the stock of the shotgun in front of him. 'This gun has never been used as a threat by me to anyone.'

Mr Cox returned to the idea of the operation being a success because Neilson had escaped from the crime scene. Neilson thrust back his shoulders and admitted his pride in carrying out the abduction and getting away with it 'scot-free' for nearly a year afterwards. Mr Cox challenged this.

'I did get away, scot-free.'

'I suppose you are proud of that.'

Neilson turned to look at the judge. 'I am proud of the fact that the plan worked, my Lord. I am talking about the entirety of it. I am not talking about in relation to the dead. That was not part of the plan.'

This was now Neilson's fifth consecutive day in the witness box and if one had to admire anything about this man it was his powers of endurance in standing there for so long giving his evidence to a murder charge. He still wore his green suit and had never asked to take off his jacket or have any breaks in the heat. However, several times during his evidence the judge had to interrupt to check him using the expression 'master plan' for the crime rather than facing the reality of what happened. But Neilson continued to regard it more as an operation than a crime and his demeanour throughout his evidence, with ramrod straight back and clipped answers, calling counsel 'sir' and referring to the judge correctly as 'my Lord', gave the impression of a military debriefing in front of superior officers. The raid had gone to plan, and the rest of the operation, as he saw it, had gone smoothly until the enemy, that is the police, had come in and started messing it up. He had told them not to contact the police and look what happened. It was obvious he wasn't to blame and he could see that the judge, as the most senior officer in court, could see it also.

'You can't bear the thought of having slipped up, can you? You can't bear the thought of any of your plans failing, can you?' asked Mr Cox.

'That's not true, sir,' replied Neilson stiffly.

'You risked causing Lesley severe mental damage by submitting her to the terrifying vision that greeted her eyes down in that drainage shaft at Bathpool Park when you first removed her blindfold. What she saw was you standing in front of her in the flickering light of a torch wearing a dark mask with two slits for the eyes.'

'That's what she would have seen, yes.'

'Do you agree this would have been a terrifying spectacle for a girl of 17?'

'In no way, sir. In no way at all.'

'Has it ever occurred to you, Mr Neilson, that you were doing this girl irreparable mental harm, quite apart from her physical harm?'

'Rubbish,' came the indignant reply.

'Did you say rubbish? Do you understand what mental damage is?'

'It may be better if you enlighten me, sir.'

Mr Cox dramatically turned his back on the accused. 'I don't think you would understand if I did,' he said.

The court went very silent as Neilson was asked to pick up the wire rope with which he tethered Lesley Whittle 60ft underground to the ladder at one end and clamped around her neck in a noose at the other. The ends were still frayed where the police had cut down her body.

He seemed reluctant at first to touch the wire and had to be urged to lift it up from the shelf at the front of the witness box and show it to the court. When he eventually did lift it up, Mr Cox asked why he had kept Lesley perpetually tethered to it, with bolted clamps that chafed the skin on her shoulders.

He said it would have been 'psychologically bad for her' to have had the wire removed. He fiercely denied allegations that he had virtually starved Lesley while she was held captive, insisting she had chosen not to eat the food provided. As to the question of how she was dressed, or not dressed, while she was underground, he said 'it was to her advantage' that she was kept naked because she always slept in the raw. He refuted Mr Cox's allegation that he'd been callously unconcerned with Lesley's welfare, maintaining instead that he'd been considerate to Lesley and that they'd been friendly, if that was possible, although he was not sure of the right word to use. He wanted her on his side because, if caught, it would have stood him in good stead with the police. Had he been cruel to Lesley, as had been suggested, he thought the police might well 'have kicked hell out of me'.

'Have you followed the newspaper and broadcast reports of the heartbreak of the Whittle family after Lesley's disappearance and the subsequent discovery of her body?' asked Mr Cox.

'I have, but I made no contact with the family, even by sending an anonymous message, because I felt the media might be co-operating with the police.'

'I suppose as those weeks passed, you were congratulating yourself on the success of your plan.'

'Indeed no, sir. The plan had not failed. The girl's death was not my doing.'

Before Neilson left the witness box for the last time after giving evidence for twenty hours, Mr Cox asked the judge if he had any questions he wanted to put to the accused. Mr Justice Mars-Jones asked him if he actually saw Lesley fall over the side of the platform. After being evasive, Neilson said, 'I did not see that happen. I did not see the act of her going over. When I say she moved forward and then to the right I am assuming that. I saw her in position as she was on the edge. I did not see her face as she went over. The difficulty is that it all happened so quickly. The head went over between the stanchion and the far wall. She slid in the bag away from the ladder. What I did see was the fact the wire went tight. She had been in a lying position, she wasn't stood up. When I said she moved, I didn't mean she walked away from me. She slid.'

29

With all the evidence now completed, the time had come for counsel on both sides to sum up their cases for the jury before the judge brought the curtain down on the trial with his summing up. The problem for defence barrister Mr Gilbert Gray QC was scratching around for something positive to say about his client to a jury who had already gasped at the audacity of this little man in the dock, posing as a military commander and boasting of his success in a plan that had gone wrong from the moment it involved anyone except 'mon capitaine' himself.

However despicable the abduction of a young girl from her bed in the middle of the night under the nose of her sleeping mother, Neilson had at least achieved this using his considerable experience as a burglar with at least 400 crimes under his belt. But once he started having to communicate with the family and organise a ransom collection, then it became apparent the directions were, at best, too complicated and at worst, unintelligible. Neilson's phone calls always came at the end of the time slots he'd arranged, the messages almost impossible to locate stuffed away behind telephone box boards, and the directions themselves obscure, at locations which were hard to find. Neilson had spent three years planning the operation, but implementation seemed last-minute and assumed that the person on the other side, usually the beleaguered Ronald Whittle, would find and understand his directions. This worked in Neilson's own family make-believe games that he carried out with his wife and daughter in the local woods, but not so well with a real enemy.

This might even work robbing post offices, where if victims didn't understand what you were saying or simply wouldn't do what you were asking, you could shoot them and that was the end of it, and congratulate yourself that you'd escaped, with or without the money. Neilson had said on more than one occasion in the Whittle trial that his biggest goal was to avoid being caught, and this he'd managed to do for nearly a year until he was picked up completely by chance by two young officers on a routine patrol. Had he shot them at once, before even getting into their car, he probably would have got away with it once again. Indeed, if he'd given up crime altogether after the kidnap he could have gone on to be a grandfather with a grandchild or two on his knee, telling tales of his military prowess to them and a wife still wondering why he never really made any money despite such military talent and ambition.

The other problem for Mr Gray was not so much his client's incompetence but his apparent cruelty and complete indifference to Lesley Whittle's fate. Here was a man with a daughter of similar age to Lesley who abducted her in a manner calculated to shock any victim into submission, keep her chained – as the judge would put it – like a dog in a dark, damp underground prison and, despite all protestations that he'd fed her and brought her little luxuries to distract her while her family delayed in handing over a ransom, let her hang herself on the end of the wire.

Lawyers are faced with the problem of representing clients who see themselves as a notch or two ahead of the game and totally blameless for the wreckage left by their efforts to make money or have a happy marriage. One way of solving this is to paint a picture to the court exactly as the client sees it, and then face the wrath of the court. The other way is to face reality and admit the incompetence of the client and then face the wrath of the client. On this occasion, Mr Gray tried to steer a delicate course between the two.

Describing his client as a lance corporal who fancied himself as a general, Mr Gray continued, 'He is the planner of military campaigns with logistics and supplies, the frustrated military man with plans ready for tactical withdrawal or strategic abandonment of the whole scheme. He is a man whose regard for his own imagined infallibility might be the envy of the Pope. You have heard of the Black Panther and Neilson; you may think this was more like the Pink Panther and Sellers.'

At this point Neilson looked over to his barrister as if he could hardly believe his ears. This was not the valedictory speech he'd expected from the man who was meant to be defending him. Whether or not Mr Gray saw the look, or perhaps sensed what his client was thinking, he qualified things a little. 'But he is certainly no Mr Average-man-in-the-street.' Although the kidnap plot and his £50,000 ransom was reprehensible and wicked, that did not necessarily make him a murderer. 'When the accused had sobbed in the dock when listening to the playback of the ransom demand in the messages from the dead girl – almost a voice from the other side – they had surely not been crocodile tears, but the emotions of a man who had never intended or desired her death. Members of the jury, I urge you to put out of your minds anger, clamouring for revenge or sense of outrage. This was unlooked for misadventure.'

Mr Gray, looking every inch the healthy outdoor man with ruddy cheeks and a deep suntan, looked over to his client, whose period in prison had left him with a ghostly white pallor so that he looked like he lived far underground in a cave, and said that there were inconsistencies in the prosecution theory that Lesley had been deliberately pushed over the platform. 'In all these dire chronicles of crime and punishment, have you heard, members of the jury, have you ever heard of or read of a hangman's ligature that has been padded and lagged and made comfortable with no less than five-feet-six-inches of Elastoplast? Have you ever heard of a scaffold with a foam mattress prepared on it for the comfort and repose of the person to be hanged? Have you ever heard of blankets being provided for warmth, brandy for sustenance, soup ready and hot for nourishment?'

The eight male and four female members of the jury looked on, some, if not all, aware of the accused saying in his evidence that he needed to keep his victim not only alive but in good humour so that she should sound relaxed in any taped message back to her family with ransom directions. When Neilson realised that he wasn't going to get the ransom, he wasn't going to need Lesley. What was he going to do then – put her back in the car and drop her off at Highley, or phone the police to say she was at the bottom of a drainage shaft with all his bits and pieces scattered around and wait for the knock on the door?

Then it was Mr Cox's turn for the prosecution. He didn't have to do much except continue the same theme. 'The decision to murder Lesley Whittle is, in my view, totally consistent with the cold, logical, military approach adopted by the accused. He was totally devoid of human feelings for Lesley and, by his own admission, had regarded his own freedom, with no risk of identification by his victim, as being of the highest priority. You might be satisfied, members of the jury, that Lesley saw her captor's face without his hood. He gave the game away when he said that the girl had once noticed he was alarmed when he said, "There must have been something in my face, in my expression."'

With counsel for both sides having completed their closing speeches, it was the turn of Mr Justice Mars-Jones to address the jury. However, before he started to discuss the evidence, he wanted to get off his chest the fact that he was singularly unimpressed with one of the witnesses: the beleaguered Detective Chief Superintendent Robert Booth, head of West Mercia CID. It wasn't the way he conducted the investigation, rather his having a go at Scotland Yard's role in all this. He said how much he deplored Mr Booth's action in using the privilege of the court to deliver a bitter attack on fellow police officers who couldn't answer back.

Mr Booth was in court to listen to the ticking off, sitting stone-faced on the police benches while the judge peered at him over half-moon glasses like a headmaster singling out the boy, a senior prefect no less, who hadn't played the game. The judge probably liked Mr Gray's earlier analogy to the Pink Panther, and might have added the comparison, although he would never say so, of Inspector Clouseau to Mr Booth.

The judge repeated that Mr Booth had nothing to reproach himself about in the investigation, but he shouldn't have brought up the subject in evidence. 'I had no warning of what he was going to say, but if I had I would not have allowed it. Be that as it may, his views are of no help to you, members of the jury, in arriving at your verdict. They are irrelevant.'

Mr Justice Mars-Jones then turned to the rest of the evidence. The judge's task in summing up a case to a jury is a tricky one. He has to present a balanced view to the jury, warning them not to set too much value on evidence that might be sensational or unreliable, to avoid bias, particularly in cases like this where they will have been aware of at least some of the details of the case through the media. Failure to do this might give rise to a successful appeal by the accused or even a retrial.

But, for one person, the prospect of listening to all this again was unbearable. Mrs Dorothy Whittle sat alone on a bench outside the courtroom, looking straight ahead and clutching her handbag closely to her, because inside the court the tapes of the last time anyone, except for the accused man in the dock, heard Lesley's voice were played again by the judge. Mrs Whittle had no wish to hear her daughter tell her mother that she was okay, when everyone now knew that she was anything but okay, in the voice described by Mr Gray as virtually a voice from the other side.

After the tapes were played the judge described Lesley's voice as remarkably calm and unemotional in the circumstances and an astonishing performance from a girl of 17 after being imprisoned for three days underground. Lesley was certainly courageous, he told the jury, but her composure could also indicate that Neilson had succeeded in winning her confidence and convincing her that she was shortly to be set free. To what extent that helped them decide whether this man had murder in his heart was a matter for them.

On this question, the judge reminded them what Neilson had said to the prosecution when asked why he'd bothered to go back at all to see Lesley when he'd decided to call the whole thing off and left the torch at the top of the glory hole with the message attached. He had replied that all he had to do was make his escape and send a DYMO tape to the family saying where she was, but it was essential he went to her. Only to take her life, Mr Cox suggested? No, he wasn't going back in a panic.

He was returning to make sure that now help was at hand she gave him a good report. Therefore it was essential that she was on his side, that she gave him a favourable report and that there was no hostility at any time.

He did get away, of course, added the judge, with his pack on his back and in the pack were his hoods and the gun and the luxuries he said he had bought Lesley to make her life easier. When it was suggested that Neilson might have got in touch with the family to tell them where she was, he'd replied that he did know of the heartache of the family, but in his mind he'd told them where she was by leaving that message on the glory hole, assuming it would be found by the police. '"I was not pleased with myself",' quoted the judge. '"But the plan had not failed. I was not responsible for her death. I did not kill her".'

Although Donald Neilson had wept the first time the tapes were played in court, he now sat immobile in the dock, his head bowed, between two warders. When he came to the wire that tethered Lesley, the judge pointed out that the length of the wire would have allowed her to reach the bottom of the shaft with a couple of feet to spare had it not snagged on the platform stanchion. 'But would you use a noose of that kind to tether a dog?' he asked, and looked long and hard at Neilson as he put the question.

On the question of law, the judge advised the jury that if the defendant deliberately pushed her so that she lost her balance and went over the side, and that was his intention, then that was clearly murder. But there was no direct evidence that he did push her over the side, although there was a lot of evidence to suggest he did not. The prosecution was relying mainly on circumstantial evidence. If they were not satisfied it was murder, then they should consider the alternative of manslaughter, which was the unlawful killing of another by a person who does not intend to kill or cause serious bodily injury. But the person charged must have done some act which a reasonable person realises would subject the victim to the risk of some harm, even if this wasn't serious harm. In these circumstances the jury may well think the act of chaining someone up on a narrow platform, alone night and day, awake or asleep, and having to move across every time the defendant came down risked harm to her. The jury might also think that a straight verdict of not guilty was not an alternative here.

There was a period of ninety minutes between the playing of the two tapes, and when it was over a female usher came out to take Mrs Whittle back into court.

Finally at 10.20 a.m. on Thursday, 1 July, the judge sent the jury out to consider their verdict. They were invited to take with them what exhibits they wished, and they chose Neilson's collection of hoods, Lesley's dressing gown, and the Elastoplast dressing Neilson had wrapped around the noose. They also took the two tape recordings of the Lesley messages and listened to these once again in the jury room.

Just under two hours later they emerged to announce that they found Donald Neilson guilty of the murder of Lesley Whittle. Mr Justice Mars-Jones congratulated them on the amazing speed with which they had assessed the evidence and come to their conclusion.

Neilson stood in the dock with his hands behind his back to listen to the verdict, his lips slightly parted to watch the jury file back into court. He looked over to them expectantly, but none were looking back at him. When he heard the verdict he swallowed, dipped his head slightly, and gave a brief frown of disbelief. Mr Justice Mars-Jones looked over to him. 'I do not propose to pass sentence on you now. There are certain outstanding matters which I must deal with first. When I have done that I shall hear your counsel and pass such sentence as I think fit and proper on counts one and two. The sentence on count three is prescribed by law.'

After these comments, Neilson turned and almost ran back down the dock stairs to the underground passage to Oxford Prison. His day's work complete, the judge stood to leave and as the rest of the court rose to watch his exit in respectful silence, a clanking of gaoler's keys was clearly heard from downstairs followed by the slam of a steel door.

When Gilbert Gray visited Neilson in his cell after the hearing he found him curled up in a corner in a pre-natal position looking utterly broken and dejected. In Mr Gray's view, he said later, he was feeling immense remorse for Lesley Whittle and her family.

There was one person missing from the court that morning to listen to the judge's summary and the verdict. Detective Chief Inspector Booth had been taken ill on the previous evening and could not attend court. The man who'd solved every murder case he'd been asked to investigate in his long career had taken it personally that the police investigation of which he was in charge had let Lesley down. But it was the supposed disloyalty he'd shown his colleagues in the trial that really upset his superiors. His fate was to be sent back into uniform to be head of the Malvern Division and no longer to be head of West Mercia CID.

The Chief Constable of West Mercia said this move implied no criticism of Booth, nor had it any connection with the Whittle case. Booth himself said he was happy just as long as he was serving the public. He had completed thirty years' service and was coming up to possible retirement in a month, after thirty commendations in his career in which he had solved seventy murders and received an MBE just two months before the Whittle kidnap. But his swansong in the witness box at the Whittle trial left his career mortally wounded, and there was talk among officers off the record that they wished an independent enquiry could be set up to resolve these issues between Booth and his colleagues.

30

The 'certain other matters' to be dealt with by the judge before he could pass sentence on Neilson for Lesley's kidnap, demanding with menaces and murder, were the charges arising from the sub-post office killings, Neilson's arrest by the two young policemen in Mansfield, and the shooting at the Freightliner depot. So, just four days after the close of the murder trial, Donald Neilson found himself back in the same court, with the same judge and barristers, but with a different jury.

Gilbert Gray, still defending Neilson even after making remarks about him being a man utterly lacking in character in the previous trial, tried pulling an interesting flanker right after the kick-off. Before the jury was sworn he made a rather unexpected suggestion that all these remaining charges not be tried but simply left on file. Mr Justice Mars-Jones at first could only say, 'Well, Mr Gray, that certainly is a most startling suggestion.'

Mr Gray then went on to say why he thought this a good idea. His view was that all the publicity surrounding the first trial would prevent a fair trial now, even if there was a postponement for a few months or

164

another change of venue. Another lengthy trial meant more pressure on public funds spent on a man who was going to serve life imprisonment anyway. 'My Lord, it is conceded that Donald Neilson is the man who caused the death of these postmasters. In the public mind and in official records there can be no lurking fear that the marauder with the brace and bit and mask and shotgun with the penchant for post offices is still at large. A further trial is unnecessary and an act of odious super vilification.'

'I suspect that the members of the families concerned would not share your view,' said the judge.

'It is not a question of this man with the feline appellation having nine lives, each one of which has to be taken from him. Saturation is not part of English jurisprudence and is something to be shunned,' replied Mr Gray.

The judge looked over to Mr Cox, for the prosecution. He said there was much public disquiet about the crimes. 'The public interest requires matters raised in this second indictment to be tried and they should not be left on the file,' he added.

'There is another very important consideration,' said the judge. 'That is the power I have vested in me to determine the length of time I can recommend that a person stay in custody. While the interests of the accused are paramount, justice demands that the trial should proceed.'

The only point on which Mr Gray did succeed was his suggestion that the shooting of Gerald Smith at the Freightliner depot should be considered separately in a different trial because it was too dissimilar from the other charges, and with this the judge agreed.

As the jury was sworn in to start the trial, the defence objected to three lady jurors, as usual not having to say why they objected, until the court ended up with an all-male jury. Mr Cox opened the case for the prosecution by saying that the statements given by Neilson on his arrest some two years after the post office robberies suggested that the gunfire was accidental. 'But time and time again what was uppermost in this man's mind was the avoidance of identification, detection and arrest and he was prepared to kill if necessary.'

After outlining the facts of the three post office raids and Neilson's eventual arrest, Cox called his first witness, Mrs Johanna Skepper, Donald

Skepper's widow. Softly, and with only the slightest tremor in her voice, she told the court how her husband died after the hooded gunman had burst into their bedroom. The judge suggested she sit to give her evidence. 'It was terrifying,' she said. 'If it had been someone whose face you could have seen, someone to whom you could have talked to reasonably ... but to see this hooded figure was very terrifying. It was so much I couldn't really have moved even if I'd wanted to get out of bed.'

She went on to describe how her husband was shot in the chest when he had a go at Neilson. She was still in the blood-soaked bed, cradling her husband's head and in a state of severe shock, when the police arrived. She only once glanced at Neilson, who was sitting just 10ft away from her, his head bowed and his eyes cast down.

Her son, Richard, was next in the box and said that the gunman had asked him to go into his parents' bedroom to find the keys to the safe. Richard hadn't agreed with his father's action to tackle the gunman, getting out of bed and saying, 'Let's get him!'

The appearance of Mrs Margaret Grayland, the village postmistress whose husband was shot dead by Neilson, was even more dramatic. She was described as a nervous wreck after the beating she received from Neilson because she'd got a sight of him without his hood. She sat sobbing in the witness box, being comforted by a policewoman and gulping a glass of water. 'We always agreed that if anyone broke in, our lives were more precious than the money. We would have handed it over if we'd had the chance.'

Instead Sidney Grayland was shot dead and she was attacked as she knelt beside him. She was found by the police nearly four hours later with multiple injuries to her head. Her husband's last words were, 'Watch it, Peg. I've been hit.' She then caught a glimpse of a man's face in the light streaming through the open door and felt a blow. Mr Cox told the court that Neilson thought he was acting in self-defence against two assailants. Mrs Grayland had needed 4 pints of blood on admission to hospital and an immediate operation.

Another postmaster's widow, Mrs Marion Anstin, described how her burly husband, although mortally wounded with gunshot wounds, still managed to grab Neilson and throw him down the stairs. Mrs Anstin was barely audible as she described her husband then slumping to the landing in a pool of blood and him dying in her arms. Minutes earlier she'd remembered her husband getting out of bed and pushing a small, black clad figure out of the door and throwing him across the landing into the bathroom. The intruder then moved forward and there was a flash as he fired his gun at point-blank range at her husband.

Finally came the two young policemen, one a former miner and the other an amateur karate expert, with their story of arresting Neilson quite by chance on the evening of 11 December 1976. The court heard how the two-man police crew on a routine patrol had stopped Neilson, who then produced a shotgun and told them to drive off with him in the passenger seat. After a twenty-minute drive they overpowered him and the shotgun had gone off, singeing them both. When they finally wrestled the man out on to the pavement they got help in subduing him from customers at a fish and chip shop.

The customers consisted mainly of Nottinghamshire miners. Keith Morris had grabbed Neilson's arms while Keith Wood, who had been trained in judo and karate, delivered a karate chop to the back of Neilson's neck, felling him to the ground. Wood, who'd injured his hand giving the blow, then placed a foot on the small of Neilson's back to stop him getting back up.

Meanwhile, several other of the customers had arrived and joined in restraining the prisoner, although accidentally several of the blows landed on the policemen. The men handcuffed Neilson to a set of nearby railings outside a public lavatory. Wood remembered one incensed onlooker going up to Neilson and giving him a gratuitous punch in the face. In the end the two police officers had to protect Neilson from further attacks from the public that had formed a melee around him about ten strong.

The prosecution closed its case with Detective Chief Inspector Walter Boreham of New Scotland Yard, who'd taken down Neilson's statement shortly after his arrest. He said Neilson had admitted it was his gun that killed three people in the post office raids, but in each case the gun had been fired accidentally. In the case of Mr Skepper, the gun had gone off when he grabbed it; with Mr Astin, Neilson had merely intended to fire a warning shot over his head but Mr Astin moved in front of his gun; and in the case of Mr Grayland, the .22 pistol had gone off as they scuffled when the postmaster tried to detain him.

After this, the trial had to be adjourned because Neilson was suffering the effects of an aggravated stomach ulcer and wasn't up to giving evidence as he had been due to do next in the proceedings. A special diet hadn't been available for him over the weekend at Winchester Prison where he was being kept during the trial. Actually Neilson then got a decent break for his ulcer as next day the building was being used by Oxford County Council and their business took precedence over the court.

31

On Wednesday, 13 July 1976, the trial resumed to hear Donald Neilson's evidence. He'd had a day and a half to rest with his stomach ulcer, but he still looked pale as he stepped into the witness box and swore the oath.

He told a hushed court how his two years' national service in the army prepared him to launch his criminal career with military planning and precision. He said he went on reconnaissance to look at various post offices with a bag of firearms, knives, camouflage clothes and cap. He'd even gone to the lengths of having a bath before each raid and wearing clothes soaked in disinfectant to put off any tracker dogs. He said it was his policy never to use road transport after a raid because once the alarm was given that would be the first place the police would look. If he was on foot they'd be looking in the wrong place.

But all the preparation hadn't prevented him being taken by surprise on three occasions while in action, and this resulted in him accidentally shooting three postmasters dead. Describing this, he became emotional and wiped a tear from his eye. He told the jury of his deep regret. 'I don't think words cover it,' he said.

He described how after shooting Donald Skepper in Harrogate he hid in a hole in woods covered by branches all the next day. After shooting Derek Anstin in Accrington he lay on a girder above a stream all day until it was evening.

He tried to explain his reason for picking on post offices; it was because he saw people in his home city of Bradford getting government benefits and he thought if he took money from post offices then all the government had to do was print more money.

Once he'd selected a target he went on a dry run. 'I went one night and spent the whole night covering the area, getting to know whether the neighbours had dogs or whether there were dogs in the surrounding areas. I checked for burglar alarms or tins of dog food or dog bowls.'

Mr Gray asked him why he carried a sawn-off shotgun, and Neilson replied that it was simply a tool of the trade – 'everyone understands you mean business when you carry a sawn-off shotgun'.

However, this appeared not to be the case when it came to the Skepper raid in Harrogate, because Donald Skepper jumped out of bed and grabbed the gun with both hands and shouted to his son, 'Go on, Richard, finish him off!' Neilson said he had clearly lost control of the situation and they weren't going to listen to a word he said. Neilson said when Skepper grabbed the gun he pulled it towards himself and the gun went off.

Gray then asked him why after this Neilson had chosen to raid another post office, this time in Accrington. The answer was simple, said Neilson, he knew what he'd done wrong, namely allowing Donald Skepper to come within grabbing distance. He'd also taken a .22 pistol with him that night to shoot at any police dogs that might try to stop him.

Here he went upstairs looking for the keys to the safe and crawled on his hands and knees across the landing. He heard some movement behind the door. 'The man jumped out of bed and in a flash he was standing there in front of me. The thought that first came to me was to get off a warning shot to startle the man or frighten him back so that I could get down the stairs. I missed the safety catch the first time I tried to release it to get off a warning shot, but managed to release it the second time. The gun was pointing somewhere up at the ceiling and I fired.'

'When you fired did you think there was any danger of the man being hit?' asked Mr Gray.

'No sir, not from the direction in which the gun was pointing. The man grabbed at my left shoulder and I went over. He spun round as I shot him. Then as I fell the .22 pistol went off. I think it was the act of my elbow hitting the ground. I did not intend to fire the gun.'

Mr Gray looked over to the jury. 'Cynics might say, Mr Neilson, that things went wrong a second time.'

'Yes,' agreed Neilson.

'Is it right, nonetheless, that on 11 November you were making your way to Langley Post Office?'

'Yes.'

'After what had happened at Harrogate and Accrington, in what way did you decide to change your equipment and technique?'

'Firstly the shotgun was not used,' said Neilson. 'But I had to have something the man could see and realise was a threat; this is why I had the .22. I also had some ammonia taped to the torch. This was for any dog that might be on the premises.'

In the struggle that ensued between the postmistress's husband and Neilson, ammonia was squirted into Neilson's eyes and the gun went off.

Mr Cox next showed Neilson an array of weapons found at his house, including two rifles fitted with silencers, a sawn-off shotgun and a steel-cored cosh. Neilson showed how he'd held a pistol when he assaulted the postmistress. 'But violence was not a thing that was planned, but it was necessary at the time,' he explained. 'It has never been part of my plans.' This reference to violence not being part of his plans brought a ripple of laughter from the court and a moment of light relief in what had otherwise been a grim account of three killings.

He agreed that the post office raids attributed by the police and the press to the Black Panther were carried out by him, but he'd never described himself as such and had not accepted the tag. 'I am myself, I am not the Black Panther,' he said.

He sobbed as he remembered his arrest the previous December. 'These policemen thought I was the Panther and in a short period I lost everything. I had lost my family and I was being accused of being a character I was not.' Neilson then dissolved into uncontrolled sobbing, dabbing his eyes with a white handkerchief. The judge watched this and suggested he might like to sit down or have a drink of water.

When the sobbing didn't stop, the judge said, 'I think we should have a break. Would you like that?'

Through his tears Neilson nodded, and the court was adjourned.

On the third day in the witness box, the prosecution tackled Neilson on his suggestion that all three shootings were accidental. 'All this talk of accident after accident in relation to all these weapons is wrong, totally wrong, isn't it?' said Mr Cox.

'I have told the court my account of what happened and this is the truth,' replied Neilson.

'I don't suggest that you set out on these criminal escapades to take life. It was probably the last thing you wanted. But when you were faced with a situation in which you had lost control of events, to protect your own skin and your own security you were prepared to take life, weren't you?'

Neilson replied that the facts of the three deaths did not bear this out. In fact at the time of his arrest he had given up raiding post offices because of the fatalities, and he was on his way to burgle private houses instead.

The Black Panther tag was taken up by Mr Gray in his final address to the court for the defence. 'The name is full of menace and stealth,' he said. 'It is feline, it is frightening. On the strength of it, Donald Neilson has been tried and convicted in every bar parlour in the country. As a professional burglar obsessed with logic, deduction and planning he might well have regarded himself as being to crime what Sherlock Holmes was to detection. But these three deaths, which my client insists had occurred accidentally, had incurred against him the gut reaction of the ignorant majority.' The Black Panther tag, probably coined by the press, was the worst of it. Neilson had consistently rejected the description.

'What he is saying,' Gray continued, 'is that he is not the mythical figure of the Panther, more full of fear than any tiger burning bright in the forest of the night. He is just a jobbing joiner from Bradford and he is a crook. He walks on two legs, even if they are crooked ones, not four. On the face of it, members of the jury, you may think the defence do not have a chance. The labours of Hercules were easy compared with their task. When Pharaoh told the Children of Israel to make bricks without straw at least he gave them a bit of clay to be going on with. You must even have thought, members of the jury, what on earth can be the defence? How can anyone, any lawyer, present any case that is acceptable in common sense? This really is mission impossible. But as this case has progressed this view might have changed. My client's claim that each of these postmasters had died accidentally because his gun went off was not beyond the realms of possibility.'

Mr Gray looked up at the jury over his half-moon glasses. 'You might say to me: "Pull the other one, it has bells on it",' he conceded. 'But earthquakes and floods relied on a similar coming together of risks, and they sometimes came in multiples: remember the old wives' tale of accidents coming in threes?

'Members of the jury, you have heard how my client was a former national service lance corporal, and was a failed carpenter who retained a love of things military. Do you remember how his face lit up when the Ordnance map for Mansfield was handed to him in the witness box? He opened the sheet out as if he was on manoeuvres. Back to the military manual seems to be his delight.

'But he was not a professional soldier. He left the army. You may think had he remained honest he would have been a good soldier because he had an enthusiasm for military preparation and detail. But he was a little man with big ideas. Not a super-criminal who went out to kill, but a burglar who bungled for all his intelligence and fascination for detail. He was not insane but showed an unbelievable irresponsibility and inability to appreciate the horrendous risks he took by setting out armed on his burglaries.'

With a flourish Mr Gray flapped the sides of his gown as he asked the jury to find his client not guilty of the murder charges and sat down. He'd done his best with what he called 'mission impossible', but you never knew. Juries were funny things, quite capable of making surprising decisions and you never quite knew until the verdict was returned.

For a prosecution with a strong if not overwhelming case the art is to keep the closing speech brief. The jury don't need convincing. Mr Philip Cox insisted that each of the three murders had been deliberate, because the postmasters, in having a go at Neilson, had threatened his personal freedom. 'You may think he was waging a small war on society. Can you, members of the jury, really accept that a man with his cunning and ability to plan so carefully would be so inept in the handling of firearms to discharge them accidentally on three occasions? In my submission, it is nonsense.'

32

In his summing-up Mr Justice Mars-Jones warned the jury not to be overwhelmed by the publicity given to a man who faced such a formidable list of charges. They would have to bear in mind in coming to a just conclusion that the accused repeatedly claimed to have been the victim of a similar accident, and one from which he personally kept his freedom when challenged during burglaries. 'You might think eight words spoken to the police shortly after his arrest could be the most telling and significant feature of all the evidence against him. Those words are "when the Black Panther shoots, he shoots to kill". If he said that, you may think it throws a flood of light on the Black Panther's activities. Although at that time Neilson was still denying he was the Black Panther, why should he say them if they weren't true? What was the point of saying them?'

The judge invited the jury to go out and consider their verdict and take with them any exhibits they wished. The jury was out for only five hours, not long for a trial of this scale and complexity, and as they filed back into court not one member of the jury looked over to Neilson in the dock. The clerk to the court then asked him to stand, which he did, with his head erect but eyes damp, like a man about to face the firing squad.

The foreman of the jury was then invited to give the court the verdicts: guilty of the murders of the three postmasters, guilty of grievous bodily harm to the postmistress, but not guilty of the attempted murders of the postmistress and the police officer.

Mr Justice Mars-Jones turned to the prisoner. 'Donald Neilson, the evidence against you was quite overwhelming on all the counts on which you have been convicted. The enormity of the crimes of which you have been convicted in my judgement put you in a class apart from all convicted murderers in recent years,' he said. 'You embarked on the ultimate in villainy in the kidnapping and holding to ransom and ultimate murder of Lesley Whittle. Whenever you thought you were in danger of arrest you showed no mercy whatsoever.

'In your case, life must mean life. If you are ever released it must only be on account of great age or infirmity.'

In passing the maximum sentences available the judge had ignored Mr Gray's request before sentencing that Neilson should be left 'with a glimmer of light in the darkness of perpetual imprisonment'. As the sentencing went on Neilson's brow creased into more of a wince. A nervous tic, which had affected the right side of his face when he was stressed through the trial, started again and the tears came into his eyes. When sentencing was finally over he almost ran back down the stairs to the tunnel back into Oxford Prison.

The further charge of attempting to murder Gerald Smith, the security guard at the Freightliner depot, was left on the file as the prosecution said that it was not in the public interest to have a third trial.

In short, everyone had had enough.

As the judge left in his official car he was cheered and applauded by the crowd waiting for him outside the court.

On appeal Neilson challenged only one verdict, that of murdering Lesley Whittle. The application for leave to appeal was heard in the Court of Criminal Appeal in the Strand, London on 1 July 1977. Neilson left the hearing up to his lawyers and did not appear. Gilbert Gray, appearing once again for Neilson, had an uphill task as there was no new evidence or argument to use, and relied on the old argument that there was no evidence of an intention to kill Lesley, and that the conviction was unsafe and unsatisfactory in that the publicity about the Black Panther had made a fair trial impossible, and that pre-trial publicity had made the jury aware of the post office killings.

Lord Justice Lane was not having it. 'On this argument, the more horrifying the crimes committed, the more likely it is that the newspapers would make a meal of it and therefore the less possible it would be for it to be tried. Nothing that the jury could have read or seen on television could have matched the horror of the evidence – oral or by photograph – which was presented to the jury in the hearing of the case.'

Lord Justice Lane commented that the trial judge dealt adequately with these points in his summing-up, telling the jury in an easily comprehensible way and there was no reason to believe the jury disregarded this. He praised the judge's summing-up as a model for any trial – concise, lucid, couched in simple language, accurate in facts and concise in law. He added there was nothing about the conviction which the Appeal Court considered to be unsafe, unsatisfactory or which raised a lurking doubt. On the question as to whether Lesley fell or was pushed, the judges felt that they too would have arrived at the same decision as the jurors.

In dismissing the appeal, Lord Justice Lane concluded that if ever there was a proper decision by a jury, it was this.

33

One person who was not in court to listen to the trial or sentencing was Mrs Irene Neilson. The question must have crossed everyone's mind as to how much she knew about her husband's activities during the three years he was planning the Whittle kidnapping and carrying out the post office raids. Donald Neilson might have been able to use the excuse that he had to be away from home a lot as a jobbing builder, but what would he do with the cash and postal orders stolen from the post offices, and why were the hours so erratic on these building jobs? Why was the income so erratic, arriving in bursts of two or three thousand and then nothing for months on end? Even if she did know what was going on, was her involvement under duress from a military man who treated her as a sergeant major might treat a new recruit?

The answer to some of these questions came on 22 July 1976 when Irene Neilson was charged at Stone, Staffordshire, with seven offences of handling stolen postal orders. She was given bail and gave her address as Leeds Road, Thornbury, Bradford, although she said she had lived at various addresses since her husband's arrest. Then, on 20 August at Eccleshall Magistrates' Court, Staffordshire, she admitted to burning forty or fifty postal orders in the hearth of the fire at her home when she saw the news of her husband's arrest on television.

The court heard that she and her husband would drive around until he selected a post office and gave her the postal orders to cash. She said she was scared and cashed eighty or ninety orders in total. The prosecution said that this was true to an extent, but she cashed some herself while her husband cashed others in the West Midlands. The Post Office had applied for £600 compensation from her for the present charges, with seventy-six other offences to be taken into account.

Irene Neilson stood in the dock wearing an orange headscarf and dark glasses while the court listened to her solicitor say that this was not a 'Bonnie and Clyde' case of a couple travelling around the countryside committing crimes in which they were equally involved. It was a case of the man – one of the most notorious criminals of the decade – who exercised a hypnotic, Svengali-like influence over his wife. 'When Neilson said jump, the whole family had to jump,' said Mr Barrington Black. 'He had served in the forces and at home became a strict disciplinarian. Even on matters of minor family behaviour, his word was law and woe betide anyone who argued with him. He was a quasi-military figure who barked like a sergeant major and told his wife and daughter what to do.'

This was the image Neilson confirmed to Mr Black when he saw Neilson in his top security cell. Mrs Neilson had no grounds for believing her husband was involved in terrifying post office attacks, and there was no question of her encouraging him to commit the offences. She played a passive part.

'Here is a woman who was forced into a situation by an evil man who had exerted an immense influence over her and for whom she had this fear in her heart,' said Black. The solicitor told the court that in the early hours of 13 December 1976 the police arrived at the Neilson home in Bradford. Mrs Neilson claimed that she hadn't any postal orders but police found a partially burned 35p postal order in the fire grate. It was one of a batch of postal orders and premium bonds worth £1,900 that had been stolen from Tittensor, Staffordshire.

'Donald occasionally goes out in the evenings and is out all night and does not come in until the following morning. I have seen him go out with a haversack during the daytime. The first time I knew my husband was going out stealing was when I saw postal orders in the living room drawers in about March 1975,' she told the police in a statement. 'On the night of Donald's arrest when Donald did not come home I got worried. When I heard the television news I put two and two together and decided to burn the postal orders in the fireplace in Donald's workroom.'

The solicitor for the prosecution said in fact the first occasion Mrs Neilson had cashed a postal order was on 22 October 1974 with an order worth £6 at Wakefield. From the end of October 1974 to the end of March 1975, the period during which the three postmasters had been killed, Mrs Neilson had been cashing in postal orders.

In mitigation, her solicitor said that his client wanted to sink anonymously into the background. He said the magistrates had a difficult task in treating the matter as an ordinary case, because of its dramatic and resounding background. 'Imprisonment would be inappropriate,' he said. 'It was easier for her to accept her husband's peremptory orders and decisions, rather than question his motivation. She was more fearful of his angry reactions if she refused rather than being caught. To send her to prison as a sop to those who yell out for her blood would be totally inappropriate.'

The bench then retired for an hour to discuss the matter over a cup of tea and a biscuit and returned refreshed but unimpressed. The chairman of the bench, Colonel Boote, said the seven offences and the seventy-six other offences asked to be taken into account were committed over a period of five months in various parts of the country, and therefore they could not have been done on the spur of the moment. 'We can only consider Mrs Neilson took a deliberate course. We take a very serious view as she knew full well what she was doing,' intoned Colonel Boote.

The sentence handed down was six months for each of the handling stolen goods charges to run concurrently, with a further six months for disposing of the postal orders for her husband – a total of one year to serve. However, the bench did not make a compensation order against Mrs Neilson, probably because they knew she couldn't pay it.

Irene Neilson watched all this from the dock, unsure what it all meant as to how long she would have to serve. She was no longer wearing an orange headscarf, but a blue headscarf over a wig and dark glasses, anxious that her anonymity be preserved. Before she had time to properly digest the sentence, she was whisked by her solicitor into a side room, and fifteen minutes later they were back in court to lodge a notice of appeal. Mr Black told the court that the appeal was against the severity of the sentence. His client was of previous good character and she had admitted the offences, which were committed at the request of her husband.

The appeal was sent up to the Staffordshire Crown Court, where Gilbert Gray surprised everyone by producing Donald Neilson himself at the hearing. Gray told the judge, sitting with two magistrates, that he wanted them to be aware of the pressure and constraints put on Mrs Neilson by her husband.

Neilson had been brought from the maximum-security wing at Leicester and gave evidence handcuffed to a prison officer. He looked pale, but otherwise fit, and gave his evidence looking at counsel and the judge, hardly taking time to look over the court to his wife. 'I was the boss at home and there was no doubt about it,' he started. 'I had a military outlook after leaving the army as far as discipline in the home was concerned, although I did not think of it at the time as being military discipline. Things had to be done when I said they had to be done. If for any reason they were not done, it was my job to enforce the discipline and see that my decision was carried out. It was shown by my attitude towards them. It had to be understood that what I said went and if this involved knocking about, it had to be.'

When asked by counsel, he agreed that his business activities always had preference. 'I tried to build up the business rather than bother about a good comfortable home, which came second to what I was trying to do. My wife had no friends and I stopped her from going out to work because I preferred her to stay at home and look after the family. I told her to cash stolen postal orders because the publicity surrounding my crimes made it difficult for me to do so. She did not know they were stolen and when she asked questions about them I told her to mind her own business.' When he'd finished giving evidence Donald Neilson was taken back to Leicester under heavy escort.

Giving his judgement at the end of the hearing, the judge said he was not impressed with either husband or wife. 'We have seen and heard Donald Neilson and rejected his testimony. We were not impressed. At the end of the day we feel that what has been said about the domination of Neilson over his wife still has about it a vagueness that we find unsatisfying and uncompelling. With every sympathy we might have for a woman before the court for the first time, these matters are serious and accordingly we dismiss the appeal. We feel the sentence was neither wrong in principle nor excessive in degree.'

Irene went on to serve eight months of her sentence before being released for good behaviour.

34

If revenge is a dish best served cold, then it had thirty years to cool off before it struck Donald Neilson.

He'd made a model prisoner, keeping up his daily regime of fitness, keeping his cell tidy and being generally friendly to fellow prisoners and prison staff. However he said he found the continual questioning from the prison staff about his intentions of escape or suicide distressing. This didn't rule out, he told a psychiatrist, the possibility of 'topping himself', as he put it, one day in the future. His efforts at denying he ever wanted to escape from prison weren't convincing.

He saw himself settling down as a lifer as his notoriety as the Black Panther died down, and possibly learning German and other intellectual pursuits. He knew he had the brains to do it and had had his IQ assessed at 119. However he'd always been wary of ordinary criminals, who were in his view work-shy and only interested in sex and didn't keep their bodies fit, and realised he'd probably have to work with his fellow prisoners if he was going to study.

Then, in 2008 he started complaining that an arm was preventing him doing his press-ups properly. He later reported difficulty getting up the stairs after meals or exercise, with eating difficulties because he couldn't seem to swallow properly. As a man who'd had so little illness or health problems during his long sentence, his complaints were treated seriously and a series of tests finally diagnosed motor neurone disease in June 2008.

Motor neurone disease (MND) is a neurological condition that causes the deterioration and loss of function of the cells in the brain and spinal cord, which control the muscles in the body. The condition is progressive and worsens over time until the patient usually dies within five years after the onset of the symptoms.

The diagnosis took place in Full Sutton Prison in East Yorkshire, a Category A and B high-security prison for some of our most violent and dangerous prisoners. In these conditions prisoners suffering from the sort of disabilities brought on by MND are not easily catered for and Neilson was transferred to Norwich Prison in 2009 which had a specialist wing better equipped to cope with him.

With the loss of control over his body movements and difficulty eating, Neilson became more and more challenging and unco-operative. For a personality that was fuelled by the control of other people, to the extent that during his crime spree anyone disobeying his orders would be shot or clubbed over the head, and for someone who had taken this infamy with him to prison and at last gained some respect as the Black Panther, this loss of control and increasing dependence on medical staff to perform everyday tasks for him made the situation intolerable.

Finally, Neilson contracted a chest infection and pneumonia, not unusual for MND sufferers, and was transferred to the Norfolk and Norwich Hospital where he died at 6.30 p.m. on 18 December 2011. At the end he made it clear to the doctors that he didn't wish to be resuscitated if he suffered a heart attack. No one from his family had come to see him in prison, or in the hospital, nor did they attend the inquest afterwards. However Kathryn sent the hospital a note after his death thanking them for looking after her father.

So, at the age of 75, Donald Neilson, after serving thirty-five years as a prisoner responsible for the deaths of two postmasters, one husband of a postmistress, a security guard and a 17-year-old girl, was dead – unloved and unmissed.

It was a sad life, tragic for his victims and their grieving families; a life spent trying to make up for his failure, failure in the army when he was back-squadded after failing his basic training, being bullied at school for being short with a silly name, a marriage in which he went to obsessive lengths in trying to control his wife and daughter, finally to lose all control over his own body through a wasting disease that left him dependent on others.

Probably the greatest compliments paid to him were from the police themselves, who marvelled at the way this one-man gang plotted and executed his crimes with such meticulous detail and foresight, apparently without an accomplice, and managed to evade arrest for ten months. Even then there was respect from the police anxious to establish it was not them who caused the injuries on his arrest, and who tolerated every answer to their questions taking nine to twelve minutes to arrive, asking him if he needed a rest or a cup of tea instead of bullying and blustering him.

Probably, with hindsight, the best thing that could have happened to Donald Neilson would have been his staying in the army after national service. He might not have made a brilliant soldier, but he was meticulous and eager to learn. Instead, he struggled to make a living in civilian life, confused as to why jobs from running a taxi to knocking up sheds in the back garden never really made him enough money, when his immigrant neighbours fresh into the country were able to find work and even pay for the house next door with a suitcase full of cash – the sort of thing he was hoping to receive from Ronald Whittle for the return of his sister.

None of it made sense to him, none of it was fair. He was born too short, he was born with a lousy name, and both meant he was bullied at school and in his beloved army. In the end they got him in the witness box with taunts of failure, his wonderful master plan that didn't work. Even the judge had to ask him to stop calling it a 'master plan'. Well, as far as he was concerned it did work because he got away with it for ten months. He got clean away from the scene even if he didn't get the money and the girl died. Her death was an accident – that wasn't his fault. Nothing was his fault.

❖   ❖   ❖

On an occasion since Lesley Whittle's death a bunch of roses was left on the drainage cover in Bathpool Park above where she was found, along with two lines from the song 'Forever Autumn':

> Like the sun through the trees you came to love me,
> Like a leaf on a breeze you blew away.

The lines remember a bright 17-year-old girl with her life in front of her, the daughter of a father who, like his father before him, spent his life building up a family business. His mistake, proving fatal for his daughter, was for whatever reason not to pay his estranged wife proper maintenance. Another man, who probably would have paid his wife nothing if he'd divorced her, felt morally outraged by this injustice and tried to take a shortcut with one final spin of the wheel, the gamble that was supposed to end his life of crime. But the ball on the wheel fell into black instead of red, and the Black Panther was finally put in a cage where he suffered a death not as terrible at Lesley Whittle's, but as prolonged and humiliating as fate would allow.

BIBLIOGRAPHY

Cooper, William, *Shall We Ever Know? The Trial of the Hosein Brothers for the Murder of Mrs McKay* (London: Hutchinson, 1971).

Hawkes, Harry, *The Capture of the Black Panther* (London: Harrap, 1978).

Lowe, Gordon, *The Acid Bath Murders: The Trials and Liquidations of John George Haigh* (Stroud: The History Press, 2015).

Miller, Gene, with Barbara Jane Mackle, *83 Hours Till Dawn* (New York, Doubleday, 1971).

Murder in Mind, vol. 18 (Marshall Cavendish, 1996).

Murder Casebook, vol. 16 (Marshall Cavendish, 1990).

Valentine, Steven, *The Black Panther Story* (London: New English Library, 1976).

INDEX

Anstin, Derek 69, 170
Anstin, Marion 69, 166

Bathpool Park, Kidsgrove 14, 50, 81
Bevington, Inspector 103,105
Black, Barrington solicitor 179
Boote, Colonel 180
Booth, DCS Robert 23–8, 77, 80,
      137–9, 159, 163
Boreham, DCI Walter 167
Brown, Dr John pathologist 135

Court venue 118
Cox, Philip QC 118

Daily Express 11, 142
Dudley Zoo 13, 30, 83

Ford, DC Andrew 137

Gray, Gilbert QC 118
Grayland, Sydney and Peggy 69

Highley, Shropshire 5, 13
Hosein brothers 72

Inskip, Paul and Simon 81

Kidsgrove 10
Krist, Gary 75

Mackenzie, PC Stuart 95, 167
Mackle, Barbara 75
Mangold, Tom 78
Mansfield Woodhouse 95, 103
Mars-Jones, Mr Justice 120
Maskery, DC 78
McKay, Muriel 72
McNaught, DS John 100
Morris, Keith 167
Morrison, Commander John 105,
      110

Neilson, Donald 9, 29
   Army training 87

Escape from Bathpool Park
59–62
Family background 89
Freightliner shooting 31–3
Evidence of at trial 140
Evidence of for wife 182
Grangefield Avenue, move to
91
In his lair 10, 12, 104
Lesley's death 57
Modus operandi 13,
Police questioning 110
Prisoner, as 183
Whittle Will 11
Neilson, Irene 10, 106, 178–82
Neilson, Kathryn 10, 93, 106

Oxford Crown Court 120

Palmer, Mrs Rosaline 99
Perriton, Sergeant 78, 136

Ransom messages 8
Readwin, DCS Roy 102, 137
Rudd, Len 47

Shorto, Peter 50
Skepper, Donald 68, 170
Skepper, Johanna 68,165
Skepper, Richard 68, 166
Smith, Gerald 31, 165
Swan Shopping Centre,
Kidderminster 27–8

White, PC Tony 95, 167
Whittle, Dorothy 5, 6, 7, 11, 23–6,
43
Whittle, Gaynor 5, 7, 23–6
Whittle, George 5
Will 11
Whittle, Lesley 5, 6, 7
Abduction 16
Death 57
Incarceration 38–42
Whittle, Ronald 5, 7
Evidence of 133
Failed Bathpool Park drop
48–52
Gloucester ransom hoax 34
Whittle, Selina 6, 11
Wood, Keith 167
Wright, DCS 113

You may be interested in …

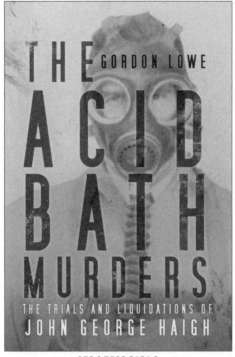

978 0 7509 6181 3

'Lowe … drives his harrowing one-sit
read with considerable narrative force.'
– *Law Society Gazette*